GOD-FOLLOWERS

Those who make a difference in the world

Study Guide 1

Larry Wade Ph.D.

WESTBOW
PRESS®
A DIVISION OF THOMAS NELSON
& ZONDERVAN

Scriptures marked KJV are taken from the KING JAMES VERSION (KJV): KING JAMES VERSION, public domain.

WestBow Press books may be ordered through booksellers or by contacting:

WestBow Press
A Division of Thomas Nelson & Zondervan
1663 Liberty Drive
Bloomington, IN 47403
www.westbowpress.com
1 (866) 928-1240

ISBN: 978-1-5127-7699-7 (sc)
ISBN: 978-1-5127-7698-0 (e)

Library of Congress Control Number: 2017903237

Print information available on the last page.

WestBow Press rev. date: 05/08/2017

A Special Thanks

A heartfelt thanks to all those who have lived a loving and compassionate God-follower life before me and my family.

Your compassion, concern and care has led us to become followers also.

Let me say thank you to all those who have been there in our times of need. You not only provided your presence and physical help, but also financial support. Some of you did without to see that we were provided for.

I would like to apologize to those whom I have failed to be there for in your time of need. I pray if that opportunity arises again, you would find me faithful.

I would like to dedicate this first study guide to my wife and children who had to endure a father who, for years, failed to live the God-follower life I knew was right.

Finally, thanks to all who encouraged me to publish a short and simple text that would be meaningful to their lives. I hope this text meets your approval.

In His Service,
Larry

Introduction

In these Life Guides we will learn about individuals who are like most of us. They entered this life the same way we did. They grew up experiencing most of the same things we do: family, school, friends, clubs, teams, dating, work, travel, marriage, children and all the in-between.

But something happened to these people. They decided to become *God-followers*. They chose to do something out of the ordinary. In fact, what they chose was so unique that it made them seem like aliens to much of the world around them.

Their change was so dramatic, even those who knew them for years could see the difference. For some, that change was so radical, it caused a wonderment as to what had taken place in their lives.

These *God-followers* were transformed into people who are pursuing a holy life. A life that they say God is calling them to. A life of goodness, love and peace toward all mankind. A life that most desire to follow. A life that can change the world into a place of *"peace and good will toward all mankind"*.

These *God-followers* are influenced by a single book and others who have committed to this life-style. Most of us have their book and have probably even read some of it.

These *God-followers* are not just readers of this book. They claim they have had a personal experience with the God of this book. They profess that God took on the form of man as a means to allow every man, woman, boy and girl the opportunity to experience the abundant life of a follower. According to biblical literature, that visible image of God was no other than Jesus Christ of the New Testament.

They believe that Jesus Christ not only lived the supreme follower life, but became the fulfillment of the sacrifice needed to atone for every individual's sins. That sacrifice provided abundant life for all, but not all choose to become a *God-follower*. They say: God came to earth so man could go to heaven. They believe prior to accepting God's plan, everyone spends most of their lives seeking the joy and peace followers enjoy.

God-followers stress reading and learning about *God-followers* of the past. *God-followers* feel this provides a channel to enter into this unique life. They propose the following experience defines or re-defines their belief. Their belief is not of working to obtain a level of holiness, but being accepted as you are and becoming what you know you ought to be. That *"ought to be"* is a life's work.

It involves failure and obstacles, joy and sadness, gain and loss. In every case, there is forgiveness and encouragement from God and other *God-followers*.

They profess there have been *God-followers* since the beginning of time. That these followers help draw others into knowledge of God's plan of love, peace and joy to all mankind.

The paradox lies in the fact, the more godly followers become, the more the unbelieving world ridicules them; even to the point of rejection and derision. Yet these followers count it joy when they are persecuted and ridiculed. Strangely enough, they accept these situations as proofs of their follow-ship.

From the historical narratives I read, the personal changes I've seen in *God-followers* throughout the years and the wooing of God in my life, I too have become a *God-follower*.

This is why I am writing these study guides. Maybe through these simple presentations you will choose to explore the Bible, investigate the lives of others, and possibly become a *God-follower*.

How to Study their book

As a whole
Analytically- in the past
Synthetically- in harmony
By the Old Testament
By the New Testament
By each Book
By each Chapter
By each Passage
By each Verse
By each Word
By History
By Events
By Example
By Biography
By Geography
By Archeology
By Topic
By Outline
By Text
By Contrast
By Character
By Author
By Theme
By Reference
By Date
By Key Thoughts
By Parallel Passages
By Illustration
By Comparison
By Exposition
By Emphasis
By Nature
By Law
By Language

Why Study their book

There is much more than just printed words to read or memorize! There is a message from God to each and every person who has a desire to experience God's Plan.

You see, their book has been presented, published, and preserved for centuries. The sole purpose of the book is to inform mankind of what life should be.

Why?
To inform those who are seeking to understand God's Plan. How to believe, how to receive, and how to acquire the joy of being a *God-follower* today.

Yes!
You can live a *"Heavenly Life"* on this earth. It all starts with not reading the book, but studying the book. It will not be easy, but every *God-follower* is admonished to study this book in order to grow in this belief.

This simple guide is written to get anyone off to a good start. It doesn't have all the answers, but will show what can be learned by using the "How to Study Method" on page ix.

We will begin at the beginning and work our way through each division of the Bible. That is the way the master teacher taught while He was on earth.

If you desire a deeper understanding of being a *God- follower*, **continue in this first guide book**.

If we are to really understand this concept, we must glean as much information concerning God's revelation of Himself to mankind as possible.

Through studying God's creation, and response to the same, we will begin to find His divine will and purpose for our lives.

By faith we will transcend centuries of change since these historical events were recorded. Through proper research and interpretation, we will be more apt to understand God's ultimate purpose and plan for His creation.

Let me encourage you to purchase at least two good reference books. We suggest a Bible Dictionary or Bible Encyclopedia. If you are not a fan of hard-copy, with modern technology, these may be found on-line.

Finally get a good literal English translation of the scripture. Not a paraphrase or modern version, just verse by verse print. I recommend the New International or New King James versions of the Bible.

You ask why? This author wants you to allow the pages of scripture, its research, and the Spirit of God to give you understanding and knowledge of the _God-follower_ principles.

I will attempt to show you how to study, verse by verse, in the divisional books of the scripture. Our first division of study will be Genesis. We will research main events and characters.

For the remainder of these studies, I will introduce each division and present a chapter summary of each section by historical structure. You should gain a good grasp of the simple truths most religious people have little knowledge of.

In these text **GFP** will stand for: _God-Follower Principle_.

This first guide presents God's first mention of re-fashioning the earth for the purpose of life as we know it today.

For the remainder of these guides, I will introduce each of the biblical books in historical narrative. I will present a chapter summary of each section. We will learn _God-follower_ concepts, characters and their actions within each story.

GENESIS

Genesis is as it states **"The Beginning"**. Genesis is to the *God-follower* what a foundation is to a house. It forms the basis for all other revelation in the Bible.

Within Genesis we cover ***five major events***.

1. **Beginning of History** (*Creation of Humankind and all earthly living things*).
2. **The Sin of Adam and Eve** (*Fall of Man*).
3. **Noah and the Flood** (*Second cleansing of the Earth*).
4. **Establishment of Nations and Languages** (*Tower of Babel*).
5. **Establishment of God-Followers** (*Patriarchal Stage*).

In Genesis we will find the **first**:

Man 1:26
Woman 2:21
Marriage 2:23
Record of fear 3:8
Curse 3:13
Promise 3:15
Thorns 3:18
Sacrifice 3:21
Birth 4:1
Death 4:8
Murder 4:8
Liar 4:9
Civilization 4:17
Person to die 5:21
Oldest man 5:27
Ship 6:14
Flood 9:11
Covenant 9:12
Tower 11:1
Languages 11:7
Prayer 15:1

As you research these sections, there may be any number of ways you would personally want to study. The main thing is that you are growing in your knowledge.

There are many people who are very interested in the information you will glean through your studies.

Your knowledge is not just facts about characters, historical settings, cultures, nations, battles, kingdoms, and religions; but encounters with those who experienced the joy of being a *God-follower*.

If you research the nuances of each of the names, places and events, you will be surprised how you can fill in the blanks of your knowledge about *God-followers*. You can share the knowledge you receive, and see the false misconceptions of those you inform erased. They might even decide to research the teaching and become a *follower* also.

*GFP: *There are periods of time in the text with no mention of God or God-followers. In many instances, all we have is a list or genealogy from father to son. No one knows why these periods exist. We can only conjecture about these times. They are apparently not important in God's presentation of His revelation or redemptive plan for mankind.*

This guide is given to present what is clearly revealed, or what is inferred comparing scripture with scripture or story to story.

DIVISIONS OF GENESIS

Genesis could be divided by **_Historical Records_**:

1. **_Creation-_** Chapter One is the beginning of *time and space (the entire universe)*.
2. **_Adam to Noah-_** Chapters Two through Eight show the *beginning of man's history*.
3. **_Flood to Tower of Babel_**- Chapters Nine through Eleven show the *moral decline* of man's history.
4. **_Abraham to Joseph_**- Chapters Twelve thru Fifty reveal a *patriarchal history* of man.

An analysis of the *periods of time in Genesis* would be:

Chapter One Unknown period of time.
Chapter Two-Eight cover a period of 1660 years.
Chapters Nine-Eleven cover a period of One hundred years.
Chapters Twelve-Fifty cover a period of four hundred and thirty years.

Genesis therefore can be divided by **numerical record** using the days of followers from *Adam to Noah*.

The following list below shows:

First the date backward from birth of Christ.
Second the date of each person's length of life.
Third the final number is their age at the birth of their first believing son.

3760 **Adam**.............930 130

> **_Cain_** *was not a follower.*

3630 **Seth**.............. 912 105
3525 **Enosh**...........905 90
3425 **Kenan**.......... 910 70
3365 **Mahalalel**.....895 65
3300 **Jared**..............962 162

3180	**Enoch**	....	365	......	65
3073	**Methuselah**	..	969	......	187**
2886	**Lamech**	....	777	......	182
2709	**Noah**	....	950	......	500
2209	**Shem**	....	600	......	100
	Ham		600		
	Japheth		600		

Ham was a non-follower.

Japheth was a non-follower.

*GFP: *Noah could have heard about creation from his grandfather Methuselah; who knew Adam for nearly two hundred years.*

The text states that Noah was six hundred years old when the flood took place. That means that the flood took place 2109 years from the Creation of Humankind *(Adam).*

God told Noah it would be one hundred twenty years until man would be judged, about the deluge that was to come, and the dimensions of the ark that Noah was to build to save those who would <u>follow God</u>.

The only ones to board the ark were Noah, his wife, his three sons and their wives. A total of eight people from the earth. God helped Noah collect a pair *(male and female)* of each living creature and an extra seven of each of the sacrificial animals needed for the time aboard the ark and once upon land.

Once the eight were aboard the ark, God closed the entry and sealed the ark for safety. The waters then began to fall from the sky above and spring forth from beneath the earth. The waters did not recede for three hundred eighty-seven days.

*GFP: *This was the* **second** *time that the waters had covered the earth. Genesis 1:2* **(HS)**

After the flood: The days of *God-followers* continued from *Shem to Joseph* as such:

2209	**Shem**	....	600	......	100
2109	**Arphaxhshad**	......	438	......	35 First person born after the flood.
2074	**Shelah**	....	433	......	30
2044	**Eber**	....	464	.....	34
2010	**Peleg**	....	239	......	30

```
1980 Reu......................239......32
1948 Serug..................230......30
1918 Nahor.................148......29
1889 Terah.................205......70
1819 Abraham............175......100
1719 Isaac..................130......60
1659 Jacob.................147......91
1568 Joseph................110......
```

Joseph was seventeen years old when he entered Egypt.

Joseph was twenty years old when thrown into prison.

Joseph was released from prison and given Asenath, the daughter of Pharoah Amenateph II, as a wife at age thirty. This was his reward for interpreting the Pharoah's dream.

Joseph was also thirty when the Pharoah made him ruler over all Egypt.

Joseph had two sons, Ephraim and Manasseh, between the first and seventh years of plenty.

*GFP: *There is much more written about Joseph than any of the previous characters in Genesis. Some consider his life a foreshadow to the life of Jesus Christ of the New Testament. Though despised and rejected by his brethren, Joseph shows mercy and delivers his family and nation.*

In all the stories of Hebrew Scripture *followers* are examples to bring us to the knowledge of the fulfillment of God's deliverance. **Romans 15:4(NIV)**

The New Testament Scriptures verify the fulfillment of God's promises of the ancient Hebrew Scriptures.

*GFP: *There were many other God-follower stories, but those chosen to be recorded were done so out of inspiration of God's Spirit. These stories show the blessing of following and the tragedy of not following God's Plan.* **John 20:21, 2 Peter 1:***21(NIV)*

Note: "Modern Earth" and Adamic existence.

From **Shem(2209) to Joseph(1568)** is seven hundred and fifty-one years.

Notes

From **<u>Adam to Joseph</u>** is twenty-nine hundred and sixty years**.**

The Exodus was **1446 B.C.** according to **I Kings 6:1** of the Hebrew Scriptures **(HS).**

1446 from 1568 = **one hundred twenty-two years**. Add those to the years from Adam to Joseph and you come up with **3082 years**.

Add thirty eighty-two(3082) and the current date twenty-seventeen (2017) and you will come up with fifty ninety-nine (5099) years from creation of Modern Earth and present mankind.

Now that we have listed a summary of Genesis from Adam to Noah; let us begin to research by peoples and events.

GENESIS AND CREATION

Genesis creation shows there is a God. One God who was at the beginning. That God was the one who made and set in order all creation. That all creation had a purpose.

*GFP: *By faith we understand that God was and is.*

Genesis 1:1 states: "In the beginning God created the Heavens(universe) and the Earth". *(HS)*

Note that there was a beginning. God was in the beginning, not multiple gods or *Polytheism*, nor no gods-**Atheism**. Note God created-not *Materialism*. God created the heavens and the earth. God was separate from His creation not *Pantheism*. Things did not just happen on their own or *Fatalism*. You do have to agree that something took place not *Agnosticism*.

There are **three heavens** known to mankind.

First, the *Atmospheric Heaven* that envelopes earth and life.

Secondly, the *Cosmic Heaven* consists of the stars, planets and galaxy's with no human life.

Thirdly, there is *Supernatural Heaven* that consist of God and other supernatural beings: angels, archangels, seraphim, cherubim.

The text mentions a group of these beings who chose not to follow God. They were therefore cast out of the third heaven. This revolt was led by Lucifer, also known as *Satan*. These beings are now known as demons within the spiritual realm. **Isaiah 14, 2 Peter 2:4, Jude 6** *(NIV)*

The biblical book of Job alludes to these beings as accusers, or those that oppose God-followers. We also have reference to their activities in the Hebrew text of Isaiah, and Ezekiel. They are mentioned in the biblical-text of Peter and Jude. *(NIV)*

It is believed by some scholars these events took place prior to Genesis 1:2. That God cleansed the earth and made it void of the first creation of supernatural habitation. These supernatural beings are no longer able to dwell upon the re-fashioned earth of Genesis 1:2. Those angels who remain in heaven are known as good angels. They are still in the spiritual realm.

The New Testament text states, God did the same to those wicked at the flood of Noah in 1656 BC from creation of Adam. He is to do the same at Christ's return to the earth, and after the Millennial Reign.

*GFP: *In every case the earth itself is not destroyed, just the creations upon the earth. We could say a cleansing.*

1. Each time the earth is replenished, not re-created.
    a. Adam was told to replenish the earth.
    b. Noah was told to replenish the earth.
2. Each time God spares the *God-followers* by a supernatural power.
3. The earth was part of original creation. It at some time (unknown) was made void of all that inhabited it.
4. This space of time between Genesis 1:1 and 1:2 some call the Gap Theory. But I don't believe there was a Gap, just an unknown time that was no longer. Therefore, God had no need to elaborate upon that time. God is giving knowledge of His "new creation". God wants mankind to know how to follow His plan for kingdom life in this age.

*GFP: *Every story in scripture is given as evidence that if you will choose goodness and forgiveness, you too will become an example of godliness.*

Basic facts that every *GOD-fOLLOWER* should acknowledge:

1. God is a Spirit.
2. The Bible is a Spiritual Book.
3. The Bible is concerned with the earthly and not the universal.
4. Humankind are spiritual beings.
5. Humankind are made in God's:

    a. **Image** (how we are fashioned or look).
    b. **Likeness** (Body/Soul/Spirit).
    c. **Clothed in Light** (glory/without sin).

6. Death is always spiritual *(unless burial* takes place).
7. Spiritual beings have eternal life.
8. Spiritual beings choose to live with God in their life or without God in their life.

HISTORICAL VERSE STUDY OF CREATION

Genesis 1:2-31 <u>Reveals the origin of all things</u>.

Creation is not scientific, but pre-science. It is not against science, but is the beginning of the physical realm of mankind as we know it. It refers to things visible and invisible.

This study reveals a progressive geocentric creation by a personal creator. This creator is not limited in time, space or material. This creator gives everything a purpose within the working of all creation. Creation is constantly moving and changing. This creation is within the realms of natural science and supernatural events.

*GFP: *Mankind cannot create, only re-purpose the created.*

Genesis 1:2 <u>Earth from the original creation is in the darkness of the waters</u>.

1. God moved upon the face of the waters.
   a. firmament, expanses above and below
   b. Energy of Motion begins

Genesis 1:3 <u>God creates light</u> or Universal Galaxies.

1. The Earth was prior to light.
2. This light is not the Sun.

Genesis 1:4 <u>God calls the Light good</u>.

1. God separates light from darkness.

Genesis 1:5 <u>God calls light day and darkness night</u>.

1. The division of the two make up a day.
   a. Night-evening.
   b. Day-morning.

The first day of creation completed.

Genesis 1:6 <u>God creates a firmament between the waters.</u>

1. Atmospheric vapors.
2. Earth's waters: salt and fresh.

Genesis 1:7 <u>God now divides the waters under and the waters above.</u>

Genesis 1:8 <u>The new firmament above he calls Heaven.</u>

The second day of creation completed.

Genesis 1:9 <u>The waters below are gathered into one place.</u>

1. Dry land appears.

Genesis 1:10 <u>God calls the dry land Earth and the waters He calls Seas.</u>

1. God said it was good.

Genesis 1:11-13 <u>God said for the Earth to bring forth grass, herbs and fruit.</u>

1. Whose seed is within itself or self-propagation.
2. God said it was good.
3. Unconscious life.

The third day of creation completed.

Genesis 1:14-15 <u>God places lights (solar system) in Heaven.</u>

1. To divide day from night.
2. For signs.
3. For seasons.
4. For days and years or time reference.

Genesis 1:16 <u>God makes two great lights and stars.</u>

1. The greater light, the Sun to rule the day.
2. The lesser light, the Moon to rule the night.
3. Stars.

Notes

Genesis 1:17-19 <u>God places lights in Heaven, both luminaries and stars.</u>

1. To give light upon the earth.
2. God said it was good.

The fourth day of creation completed.

*GFP: *God created everything needed for life. God knows what we need. Where He guides... He provides.*

Genesis 1:20-23 <u>God creates fowls along with salt and fresh water creatures.</u>

1. Fowls for earth's atmosphere.
2. Creatures for the Seas.
3. Self-multiplying conscious life.
4. God said it was good.

The fifth day of creation completed.

Genesis 1:24-25 <u>God creates beasts, cattle, creeping things and man on earth.</u>

1. Animal creation with seed within itself.
2. Beast are non-domesticated and violent.
3. Cattle are for domestication and non-violent.
4. God said it was good.

Genesis 1:26-30 <u>God creates homo-sapien or mankind.</u>

1. "Let us." (Triune image of Father, Son and Holy Spirit).
2. Likeness-as he sees us, or physical appearance.
3. Eternal existence.
4. Without knowledge of good and evil.
5. Given dominion over unconscious and conscious life.
6. Created male and female (ADAM/ADAMAH). To subdue and replenish and multiply the earth.
7. Mankind was able to eat all vegetation and fruit.
8. Beast, fowls, and creeping things were able to eat vegetation.

Genesis 1:31 God saw that everything was <u>very good</u>.

The sixth and final day of creation completed.

*GFP: *Mankind is the only creation that has God's likeness. We were created to fellowship with Him and help Him take care of His creation. Not destroy it! Within the preceding verses we see the formalness of creation. We will not gain the fullness of God's Plan until we cultivate the life of a Follower.*

Genesis 2:2 <u>God rested</u>

   1. Ceased from creating.

The *seventh day*

*GFP: "This is not a day of creation". *Even God rested from His work. We should not make work our god. Constant work brings about early death. Add days to your life, don't subtract them.*

DETAIL OF CREATION

Genesis 2:3-6 <u>Detail of Creation.</u>

1. Blessed the seventh or Sabbath day.
2. Gives generations of heavens and the earth.
3. Explains what the earth was like prior to man.
   a. No tilling of the ground.
   b. No rain.
   c. There was a mist that came from the ground and watered the earth.

Genesis 1 and 2 These chapters do not contradict each other. Chapter 1 is defining the entire story of creation as it took place *(the facts)*. Chapter two is describing the first 6 days of creation in summary, (the process).

Genesis 2:7-24 describes the separate events that take place in the Garden of Eden. God had already filled the earth with animals, birds and vegetation prior man's creation. Now God lets Adam name these other creations to let him see there was no suitable mate for him. He was alone!

God showed Adam he was the creator by giving him Eve.

Eve will:

1. Fulfill Adam's loneliness or <u>emotional needs</u>.
2. Allow pro-creation or <u>natural needs</u>.
3. God tells Adam what <u>is</u> suitable to eat.
4. God tells Adam what <u>is not</u> suitable to eat.

*GFP: *Eve cannot fulfill Adam's spiritual needs. God is a spirit and we must commune with Him spiritually. Only God can fulfill spiritual needs.* **John 4:24 (NIV)**

*Key note: The Garden of Eden is near the Caspian Sea.
     (See this on the Map provided in the appendix).

ADAM CREATED BY GOD

Genesis 2:7 <u>How man became a living soul.</u>

1. God breathed life into his nostrils.
2. We are a tri-partite being.

We are given a **body** which is <u>PHYSICAL</u>.

    a. It is visible
    b. It is natural
    c. It is ephemeral

We are given a **spirit** which is <u>MENTAL</u>.

    a. It is spiritual
    b. It is moral
    c. It is experiential

We are given a **soul** which is <u>ETERNAL</u>.

    a. It is relational
    b. It is supernatural
    c. It is euphorical, or not of this world.

*GFP: *We are influenced by each of these distinct portions of our being. How we are influenced and to what extent each part controls us is what we call PERSONALITY.*

It should be noted that mankind is recognized or defined by his spirit. Everything one does is based upon his/her moral concepts... how and what we believe. Mankind's choice to follow God is not a physical change. It is a moral change due to experiencing a personal supernatural relationship with God.

Mankind is not judged eternally for their physical actions, but for their moral choice to reject God's love, mercy and forgiveness for such actions.

*GFP: *We still suffer the consequences of our choices.*

This author has developed a list of some of the things, within human nature, that seem to influence personality.

1. **Environment**
   a. Family structure
   b. If both parents are in the house
   c. If only one parent in the house
   d. Birth order
   e. Number of siblings
   f. Type and location of house

2. **Economics**
   a. Dual or single income family
   b. Assets and liabilities
   c. Type of job
   d. Stability

3. **Education**
   a. Academic or vocational
   b. Continuing or static
   c. Desired or undesired

4. **Experiences**
   a. Positive or negative
   b. At what age experiences happen
   c. Amount of encouragement/discouragement

5. **Emotions**
   a. Expressed or unexpressed
   b. Controlled or uncontrolled
   c. Involvement with others

6. **Epistemology** (the science of knowledge, origin and validity in relation to human experience).
   a. Where did I come from?
   b. Why am I here?
   c. Is there life after physical death?

Genesis 2:8-14 <u>Garden of Eden.</u>

1. God planted it. Eden was known by Moses.
2. A <u>Tree of Life</u> which had twelve monthly leaves which provided for sustenance for eternal life.
3. A <u>Tree of knowledge</u> of good and evil.
4. A river with four tributaries.
   a. **Pison**-coast of the Caspian Sea
   b. **Gihoh**-coast of the Caspian Sea
   c. **Hiddekel**-in the land of Assyria
   d. **Tigris/Euphrates**-in the land of Babylon

Genesis 2:15-20 <u>Man placed in the garden.</u>

1. Mankind was restricted from the Tree of Knowledge of good and evil.
2. God did not want mankind to be alone.
3. All animals and Adam were formed from the ground.
4. Adam allowed to name the animals.

*GFP: *This restriction was probably set until Adam could develop his spiritual life by walking with God. It is harmful to gain knowledge of evil prior to understanding truth and goodness.*

Genesis 2:21-22 <u>Creation of a help meet.</u>

1. God surgically removed a rib from Adam.
2. God closed Adam's flesh.
3. God took the rib and made a female.
4. God took her to Adam.

*GFP: *Woman came from man, not the ground.*
Woman was a gift to man.(#4 above)

Genesis 2:23 <u>Adam's pronouncement.</u>

1. God called man and woman Adam(*red*)like clay.
2. Man and woman are equal in divine essence.
3. Man(Ish)and woman(Ish'ah)have equal names.
4. They are equal in physical essence, one flesh.
5. Woman is equal to man, but different in sexuality. (For the purpose of pro-creation).
6. Though equal, they are not interchangeable.

Notes

*GFP: *Men should be the example of godliness and provider of substance. He is to love his wife as he does himself. Women are to encourage their husband and create a relationship drawing them together for sexual encounters. This will produce a FAMILY. Women should not give such love to her children. There is a different love for family. If either fail in their duty, bitterness, strife, and divorce is certain.*

Genesis 2:24-25

**Key Note: <u>Added by inspiration of Moses.</u>

1. They are to leave father and mother.
2. They are to cleave one to another.
3. They were both naked and ashamed.
   a. They were initially clothed in light or glory.
   b. They did not know of their nakedness until they disobeyed God.
   c. Apparently, the Serpent told them. Gen.3:11*(HB)*

Genesis 3:1 <u>The Serpent Beast.</u>

1. He was Subtle or crafty.
2. He <u>*misquoted*</u> God's word, saying "every tree".

Genesis 3:2-3 <u>Eve's response.</u>

1. She <u>*added*</u> to God's Word, saying, "touch it".

Genesis 3:4-5 <u>The Serpent's half-truths.</u>

1. She would not die physically, but spiritually.
2. She would be like Satan's gods, self-made.

Genesis 3:6 <u>Eve chose not to listen to God.</u>

1. Eve was tempted by <u>desire</u>-good for food.
2. Eve was tempted by <u>eyes</u>-looked good.
3. Eve was tempted by <u>pride</u>-would make her wise.
4. Eve <u>became a tempter</u> and gave to her husband.

*GFP: *Adam had been instructed by God not to eat from the tree. He disobeyed God. Eve had been instructed by Adam but chose to listen to the serpent instead of Adam.*

*GFP: *One of the most often listed causes of divorce is when a husband or wife seeks advice from someone other than their mate, especially someone of the other gender. Couples should always keep communication open. It's hard to complain to a mate, but it is better than unfaithfulness or divorce.*

Genesis 3:7-8 <u>Loss of innocence.</u>

1. They knew they were naked. <u>The glory was gone.</u>
2. They knew they were guilty. <u>The knowledge of evil.</u>
3. They both were ashamed of their disobedience. <u>The knowledge of goodness.</u>

*GFP: *The choices we make shows the need for a better plan for our lives.*

Genesis 3:9-13 <u>God always seeks fellowship.</u>

1. God calls.
2. God knows our position. <u>Where we are.</u>
3. God knows our condition. <u>What we've done.</u>
4. God questions to help us so we realize <u>what got us to each place in life.</u>
5. Mankind always tries to <u>blame others.</u>

*GFP: *Those voices, in our head asking us to consider doing good, are God's spiritual advisers. You can tell the good voices from the evil voices, by understanding that God's advisors would never ask us to do wrong. Hence! we say "godliness" or "wickedness".*

Genesis 3:14-15 <u>Serpent cursed for what he did to Adam and Eve.</u>

1. The serpent was cursed above all *beasts*.
2. The serpent was to crawl upon its belly from that point.
3. God put hatred of the serpent's seed against the <u>seed of Woman</u> or a prophetic promise of a deliver.

*GFP: *Eve's seed was to be bruised. Satan's seed was to be wounded in the head.*
Genesis20:10(HS)
Eve's seed means that there would be a Woman, in the future, that would give birth without the seed of a man (virgin birth). This has only been recorded once in all history. The birth of Jesus Christ in Israel.

Genesis 3:16 <u>Curse of the woman.</u>

1. The woman's child-bearing was to be sorrowful.
2. The woman given desire to please husband.
3. The woman shall be ruled by husband.

Genesis 3:17-19 <u>The curse of mankind.</u>

1. They were not able to eat of the tree of life.
   The death process began.
2. The man now must labor for food. <u>Our judgment.</u>
3. The ground was cursed because of Sin. <u>Thorns and thistles now created</u>.

Genesis 3:20 <u>Adam re-names woman EVE.</u>

1. She is to be mother of all mankind.
2. In the Hebrew Language, EVE means life. Now creation is in the image of Adam and Eve. Genesis.5:3 *(HS)*

Genesis 3:21-24 <u>Man was driven from the garden.</u>

1. God covered their nakedness.
2. A blood sacrifice was needed to cover Adam and Eve's sin.
3. God kept them from living in sin forever by eating from the tree of life continually.
4. God protected the Garden from man's re-entry.
   a. Guarding Cherubim, a high order of the angels.
   b. By placing a flaming sword at the entrance.

*GFP: *The grace of God leads to the understanding of redemption. God sometimes protects us from evil. But when we do evil things, God's grace allows forgiveness.*

BEGINNING OF PRO-CREATION
FIRST OF NATURAL BORN MANKIND

Genesis 4:1-2 <u>The Generations of Adam.</u>

1. Adam and Eve conceive of their seed.
2. They have twins.
    a. Cain-a tiller of the ground.
    b. Abel-a keeper of sheep.

Genesis 4:3-5 <u>The Process of time is:</u>

1. Is a specific or designated time.
2. Cain brought <u>his</u> sacrifice, which was not respected.
3. Abel brought <u>God's</u> sacrifice, which was respected.

Genesis 4:6-7 <u>No reason for Cain to be mad.</u>

1. Cain knew what was expected by God.
2. Cain chose to be disobedient.
3. Cain had the right to rule over Abel.
    a. He was the elder brother.
    b. He had the birth-right.

Genesis 4:8-12 <u>The first murderer.</u>

1. Cain's jealousy leads to murder.
2. Abel's blood cries out to God.
3. Cain was cursed as tiller of the ground.
4. Cain was sent away in shame, to be a vagabond.

*GFP: *Within this story, as in many stories, we have something called INFERENCE. This means: the process of deriving a conclusion from later facts or logical consequences or to deduce. Cain brought what he felt was better than what was required. Sometimes by not doing what is required, we cause great harm; either to us or others.*

Genesis 4:13-15 <u>Cain asked for mercy.</u>

1. Cain feels if others, *in the future*, know what he had done, they will seek to kill him.
2. God places a <u>visible mark</u> on Cain. Probably his face so all could see easily.
3. God also warns that a greater curse would be on the person who kills Cain.

*GFP: *Cain ask for mercy, but shows no remorse. He never expresses regret. Maybe this is why he is turned away and became a non- follower. That principle seems to be in effect today. If we are not sorry for what we have done; we too often turn away from godliness.*

Genesis 4:16-18 <u>Non-followers leave the presence of God.</u>

1. Cain goes east of Eden, to what Moses knows as Nod. See the appendix maps.
2. Cain finds a wife. One of the many daughters of Adam and Eve.
3. Daughters often were not listed in man's Lineage. Because they would marry and her family name would change.
4. Cain has a son he names Enoch.
5. Cain builds a city he also names Enoch.
6. The generations of Cain begin. There is no list of ages at birth or death.
7. Cain dies during the flood of Noah.

*GFP: *Remember that Adam and Eve lived to be in their nine-hundreds. They had time to produce other sons and daughters. They also lived lives of longevity anywhere on the earth. Many of their names are recorded, also up until this time there was no written prohibition on marriage. Cain would have married a sister, a niece or a distant* relative. *Marriage had to start somewhere.*

Genesis 4:19-24 <u>Lamech's choices are worse than Cain's.</u>

1. Lamech starts the practice of polygamy.
2. Lamech is a double murderer.
3. Lamech lists his shame and his reward.

*GFP: *People know what type of lives they live, and what they truly deserve. But through God's redemptive grace man can be forgiven.*

Genesis 4:25-26 <u>Another *appointed son* in place of Abel.</u>

1. Seth begins a new seed of *God followers*.
2. Seth was born in the image and likeness of Adam and Eve. (<u>Not in Gods image</u>).
3. Seth was born with a heart that had the concept of good and evil.
4. When Seth's son Enos was born, man began to seek to follow God again.

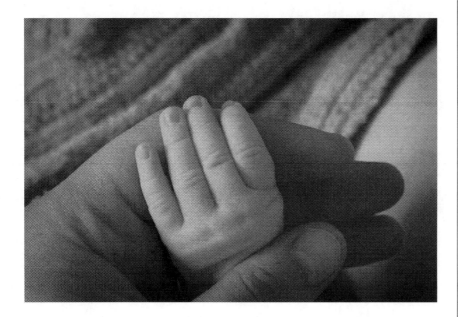

GENERATIONS OF ADAM

Genesis 5:1-32 <u>Adam to Noah's sons.</u>

1. **v. 24** states that Enoch was taken by God.

*GFP: *The Hebrew Scripture does not record his death. This is the first mention of translating someone to Heaven to be with God. Throughout history God-followers promote the teaching that, in the future, all God-followers will be translated to heaven.*

GROWTH OF POPULATION AND GROWTH OF WICKEDNESS

Genesis 6:1-2 <u>The *sons of God,* (God followers), take wives of Cain's non-following daughters.</u>

1. They took wives. They were not given.
   a. They were virgins or married.
   b. They married as many as they desired.
      1. Polygamy continues.
      2. Incest begins.
      3. Adultery begins.

*GFP: *This seems to be the common way of man world-wide. God-followers can come from any of these choices. But God-followers adhere to the biblical teaching of being the husband of one wife. They feel polygamy, incest and adultery are not in God's plan for good.*

Genesis 6:3 <u>God numbers man's days.</u>

1. God allows only one hundred twenty years for repentance.
2. Noah was warning mankind as a witness.

Genesis 6:4 <u>Giants from Cain's line co-habited</u> with daughters of non-God Followers.

1. Daughters of men bare children of them.
2. Some are giants.
3. They were great warriors
4. They were known everywhere.

*GFP: *These are not Angels: The Bible states that Angels are neither male or female, nor are they married. Matt.22:30* **(NIV)** *There is still a remnant continuation of these giants today (DNA). They exhibit extreme height and facial structure. These giants do not usually live past fifty years old.*

I personally knew the Giant Max Palmer of Mississippi. He was Eight feet two inches tall at his death in 1984.

Genesis 6:5-6 <u>Man's wickedness also grows.</u>

1. Through their imaginations.
2. Through their hearts thoughts.
3. They were evil continually.
4. God was grieved.

*GFP: *If we fill our minds with wicked thoughts and deeds, it influences our hearts. Once our hearts are changed, we begin to explore the realms of these thoughts.*

Genesis 6:7 <u>God makes plans to cleanse the earth again.</u>

1. God felt sorrowful His creation chose not to follow His earthly plan.

*GFP: *We can cause God to feel sorrow over the rejection of his love. Throughout scripture we read of God's attributes. He passed those same attributes on to us.*

Genesis 6:8-9 <u>But Noah found grace in the eyes of God</u>

1. Noah was a just man.
2. Noah was perfect in his generation.
3. Noah walked with God as a *God-follower.*

*GFP: *Meaning Noah confessed his sinful nature and his need for God's ability to make him complete or perfect. Example: Any object is not perfect until all the parts are completed. It might not be perfect in the eyes of others, but it is in the eyes of the creator. Each creation may consist of different parts, but if all that is required to complete that creation is used, it is perfectly finished.*

*GFP: *God is watching each of us on earth. He is searching for God-followers to prevent the waywardness of mankind.*

Genesis 6:13-8:18 <u>The message for Noah.</u>

1. God told Noah to build an Ark.

2. It was to be four hundred fifty feet long, one hundred fifty feet wide, and seventy-five feet high.
3. The ark was to have three levels, and built like a barge of today.
4. The ark was to have one window and one door.
5. God told Noah He would destroy all flesh.
6. God makes a covenant with Noah.
   a. God would spare Noah's family.
7. Noah was to bring in plant life for food.
8. God informed Noah that rain would come.
   a. There had never been rain before.
   b. A mist came up from the ground.
9. God caused two animals, male and female, to enter the ark.
10. God caused seven animals, he declared clean, to enter the ark for sacrificial purposes during the time aboard the ark and once out of the ark.
11. Noah and family enter the ark.
12. It rains for forty days and forty nights
13. Great winds caused subterranean water to be drawn from beneath the earth.
14. The waters stopped after one hundred forty days.
15. The Ark rests atop Mt. Ararat in Turkey.
16. Mountain tops were seen after 10 months.
17. Noah sends out a raven that never returns.
    a. Could live off any thing floating.
    b. Ravens are carnivorous.
18. Noah sends a dove that returns.
    a. There was no vegetation for the dove to survive.
19. Noah sends the dove seven days later. It returns with an olive branch in its beak.
20. Noah sends the dove seven days later. It never returns.
21. Thirteen months and one day after the beginning of the flood, the waters were dried from the earth.
22. Fourteen months and twenty-seven days after entering the ark, Noah, his family, and all animals exited the ark.

*GFP: *God always gives clear instruction for the task He expects us to perform. We should never make life-changing decisions until we are sure that God has instructed us, on how it should be done, given the provisions to start the task, and He has made the first move on our behalf. God will never ask us to do something just to prove we are a follower. God moves us by love, not peer pressure.*

Notes

Genesis 8:19-22 <u>Noah worships God.</u>

1. Noah builds an altar.
2. Noah sacrifices the required clean animals.
3. God is pleased.
4. God promises not to flood the earth again.
5. Seasons/Days/Nights shall not cease.

Genesis 9:1-19 <u>Noah is given Laws of the Earth.</u>

1. They were to replenish people on earth.
2. Creatures are now fearful of man.
3. Mankind may eat anything that does not have blood.
4. Punishment for *murdering* animals.
5. Capital punishment for *murdering* people.
6. Rainbow a token of *Noahic Covenant*.
7. Noah's sons and grandson by Ham.

*GFP: *Murder means pre-meditated killing.*

Genesis 9:20-29 <u>The Wickedness of Ham toward Noah.</u>

1. Noah becomes drunken and naked.
2. Ham violates his father.
3. Noah curses Ham's lineage with servitude.
4. Noah lives one hundred and fifty years after the flood.
5. Noah lives a total of nine hundred and fifty years.

NOAH'S GENERATIONS IN THEIR NATIONS

Genesis 10:1-32

    a.   **Shem's sons**-Israelites through Abraham the God-follower.

    b.   **Ham's sons**-not God-followers.
>   Cush-*Ethiopians*
>   Mizaram-*Egyptians*
>   Phut-*Africans*
>   Canaan-*Canaanites*
>   Nimrod-*Babylonians* and *Assyrians*
>   Sidon-*Phoenicians*
>   Heth-*Hittites*
>   Jebus-*Jebusites*
>   Pilistim-*Philistines*
>   Sin-*Orientals*

    c. **Japheth's sons**-not God-followers
>   Gomer-*Germans*
>   Magog-*Russians*
>   Madai-*Persians*
>   Javan-*Greeks*
>   Tiras-*Italians*
>   Togarmah-*Armenians*
>   Tarshish-*Spainards*
>   Kittim-*Cyprians*

*GFP: *All historical records tend to authenticate the heritage of each countries to these names. The Bible also references the usage of these names.*

Notes

THE RESULTS OF THE FLOOD

1. The Earth purged of wickedness.
2. Ice Age.
3. Moved man west.
4. Races established through the sons of Noah.

The flood was caused by the water canopy (firmament) surrounding the earth, falling upon the earth, and the underground water sources (firmament) coming to the earth's surface. The culmination of the two caused a complete global-cooling event.

The event of the rapid cooling of the earth caused the Ice Age. The cessation of the heaven's waters along with the rapid receding of the earth's waters caused the movement of animal and plant-life to be transported from one continent to another. Therefore, there are sediment layers stacked one atop the other.

__Example:__ Mammoth elephant's remains found in Wakulla Springs, Florida. Sea creatures found in the deserts of Arizona. Remains of fossils giving birth and eating. Older creation atop more recent creation.

***GFP:** *This is the author's rebuttal of The Modern Theory of Evolution.*

Dr. Willard Libby of the University of Chicago developed the use of Carbon 14 dating. It should be noted that he stated the use of **Radiocarbon Dating** was only accurate for dating objects that are a few thousand years old. Every object and person contain carbon.

There are many reasons for such a statement. Here are just a few.

1. Science indicates to us that the amount of C14 in the earth's atmosphere is increasing.
2. Science indicates that C14 has not reached Equilibrium. Therefore, the Earth is young; approximately 10,000 years old.
3. Scientific research has shown that the same object tested can reveal several different C14 dates.

4. Science has determined that geological studies show older layers of sediment are often found above younger sediments.
5. Evolution is based upon a geological column that only exists in textbooks. Not scientific evidence.
6. Each of the purported scientific finds of early man: Neanderthal (1856), Java (1891), Piltdown (1912), Peking (1912). All these have been proven to be hoaxes.
7. If man evolved from one species into man of today, Where are the different changing creatures that man was evolving into. Secondly, where are the creatures that man has been evolving into for the last ten thousand years? There is only one truthful scientific answer. Mankind was created as we are today and genetics have made the only change.
8. Animals and plants were created as one species. Genetic changes such as cross-breeding and pollination has caused innumerable types of each of these original species.
9. Biologically the oldest recorded trees and ocean reefs are less than five thousand years old.
10. Erosion with a rate of four to five feet annually indicates earth's age at less than ten thousand years.
11. Examination of mineral influx show the earth at less than ten thousand years old.
12. Flowstone formations show less than five thousand years of formation.
13. Astronomically, the rate of the galaxies cluster expansion seems to be less than ten thousand years.
14. The existence of space dust indicates a young solar system.
15. The decaying magnetic field limits the age of the earth to less than twenty-five thousand years.
16. Meteorite fossil remains are only found in the top layers of the earth surface, making them exposed less than a few thousand years.

Much more information can be found online at:

Museum of Earth and Life History, Liberty University
Institute for Creation Research, El Cajon, California
Creation Resource Foundation, El Dorado, California

Notes

THE DIVISON OF LAND AND LANGUAGE

Genesis 11:1-4 <u>The Tower of Babel.</u>

1. Populations migrated east to Mesopotamia.
2. Mankind wanted to build a city to become one great ruling people.
3. They wanted to do as they pleased.
4. They wanted to make a name for themselves.
5. They wanted to build a tower to reach heaven.
6. They wanted to be their own God or gods.
   (Astrology began atop this tower.)

*GFP: *Isn't it strange that these same principles caused the downfall of many historical peoples and nations. We should learn from evil principles.*

Genesis 11:5-9 <u>God stops man's imaginations.</u>

1. God confounds their language.
2. God begins other languages.
3. The work on tower ceases.
4. People begin to scatter across the earth by language groups.

*GFP: *We usually adopt the attributes of those most like us. We feel safe around those who look and speak as we do.*

THE GENERATIONS OF SHEM

Genesis 11:10-26 <u>From Shem to Terah.</u>

Genesis 11:31-32 <u>From Terah to Abram.</u>

1. Terah has three sons: Abram, Nahor and Haran.
2. Haran died before Terah his father.
3. Terah take his sons Abram and Nahor along with his nephew Lot, Haran's son, to Canaan.
4. On the way to Canaan, they stop in the area where Haran was born. This city is located north of Canaan in Syria. It is called Ur of the Chaldees after Ur of Persia.
5. They remain here until Terah dies at age two hundred and five.

*GFP: *It took generations to wipe away the many effects of wickedness from man. Yet centuries later it still exists.*

God wants us to purify each other, not pollute our lives.

Notes

ABRAM'S LIFE
1 FAITH FOLLOWER PATRIARCH

Genesis 12:1-20 <u>God speaks to Abram.</u>

1. God ask Abram to leave this wicked land.
2. God made a covenant with Abram of Mesopotamia.
   a. God would make of him a great nation.
   b. God would bless him.
   c. God would make his name great.
   d. God would bless those who blessed him.
   e. God would curse those that cursed him.
   f. God would bless everyone through Abram.
3. At age seventy-five Abram follows God's direction.
4. Abram takes his wife Sarai and nephew Lot.
5. Abram takes all his family that would become *God-followers.*
6. They traveled south toward Canaan.
7. They stopped in the city of Sichem.
8. God announces He will give him this land.
9. Abram builds an altar there.
10. Abram moves on to Bethel.
11. Abram builds an altar there.
12. Abram journeys southward because of a famine.
13. Abram decides to go into Egypt.
14. Due to Sarai's beauty, he tells her to say that she is his sister. He thought the Egyptians would want her and possibly kill him to take her. But if she was his sister, they would treat him well in order to purchase her from a brother.
15. The Pharaoh desires Sarai.
16. The Pharoah gives Abram many gifts for Sarai's sake.
17. God plagues Pharoahs house to warn him over his desire for Sarai.
18. The Pharoah calls Abram, finds out that she was his wife and sends them out of Egypt.
19. The Pharoah gives Abram and Sarai safe passage.

*GFP: *Even non-followers have had moral principles since the beginning of time. Many of these non-followers seek to please this God they have not come to experience personally.*

Covenants are:

Conditional- depends upon receiver's actions, <u>if you</u>.

Unconditional- depends only on the one making the Covenant, <u>I will</u>.

The Covenants of Genesis are:

1. *Adamic*.............. 3:14-19 For a redeemer.
2. *Noahic*............... 8:20-9:27 Due to a promise.
3. *Abrahamic* .... 12:1-3 Due to being *God-followers*.

The Prayers of Genesis are:

1. *Abraham* for a son 15:1-6
2.   for Ishmael 17:17-21
3.   for Sodom 18:20-
4.   for Abimelech.......... 20:17
5. *Eleazer* for a wife for Isaac...... 24:12-14
6. *Isaac* for his children.............. 25:21-26
7. *Jacob* for blessings 32:9-3

Genesis 13:1-18 <u>Abram and Lot's feud over the land.</u>

1. Abram moves back to Bethel.
2. Abram and family now rich with cattle.
3. The land could not feed Abram, Lot and all the locals.
4. Abram did not want strife, so he asked Lot to choose the land he desired. Lot chose Jordan, a rich and fertile land, even today.
5. Abram stayed in Canaan.
6. The wicked city of Sodom was in Jordan.
7. God tells Abram that he should have and fill all the land, with his descendants. Abram goes to Hebron to live.

8. Abram builds an altar there.

*GFP: *It should be noted; Abram always wanted a place to meet with God. It has been said; "A family altar, will alter a family".*

Genesis 14:1-14 <u>Lot was taken in warring.</u>

1. Shinar=Babylon
   Eleazar=Southern Mesopotamia
   Elam=Elamites
   Tidal=Hittites
2. War began against all cities near the Dead Sea.
3. After a revolt against Chedorlaomer King of the Elamites. Chedorlaomer smote all his enemies at Siddim, said to be the place of asphalt pits. Lot was among those captured.
4. Someone who had escaped during the battle came and told Abram.
5. Abram armed three hundred and eighteen warriors and pursued them up to Syria. He brought back Lot his family and all his goods.
6. The King of Sodom and Melchizedec, King of Salem, came to meet Abram, because he had overcome Chadorlaomer and all the Kings that were with him.
7. Melchizedek was also a priest of the Most High God. Melchizedek blesses Abram and tells Abram that it was God who had delivered him from his enemies. Abram gave a tithe or 10% of all he returned with.
8. The King of Sodom asked only for his people back. He told Abram to keep the bounty, but Abram said he would not take anything. For then the King of Sodom would later say that he had made Abram rich.
9. Abram asked for a portion of the goods to be given to his captains.

Genesis 15:1-17 <u>Abram asked God for a gift.</u>

1. Abram tells God that he has no heir.
2. He wonders if his steward Eliezer from Damascus would be his heir.
3. God tells him to look at the stars and and imagine them being his seed.
4. Abram asked how he will know.
5. God tells Abram to make ready sacrifices.

6. When the Sun was going down, Abram fell into a deep dark sleep.
7. God assures Abram that his heirs will live in a land, originally not theirs and be afflicted four hundred years. God would judge that nation until they would be let go with great substance.

*GFP: *You should be willing to pay the price of success. Success is not cheap. If it is, it's not worth much.*

8. That Abram would die in peace as an old man.
9. But in the fourth generation they would be in bondage because of the Amorites.
10. Then the sun went down and a burning lamp passed between the sacrifice pieces.
11. Abram does not tell Sarai.

Genesis 15:18-21 God makes a covenant "to" Abram

1. Abram is given the land from the Nile of Egypt to the Euphrates River of Iraq.
2. Abram would rule over the people of those Lands.

Genesis 16:1-6 Sarai's Mistake.

1. Sarai had not gotten pregnant and now was past normal child-bearing years.
2. She tells Abram to take her Egyptian handmaid Hagar to bare him an heir.
3. It has been ten years since God's promise to Abram, so he listened to Sarai.

*GFP: *Jealousy is the number one thing to destroy personal relationships. But lack of patience is the culprit which often breaks our relationship with God.*

4. At eighty-five Abram gets Hagar pregnant.
5. Sarai says she was wrong and Hagar seems to look down on her.
6. Abram tells Sarai to do as she pleases.
7. Sarai now deals harshly with Hagar, to the point that Hagar runs away toward Egypt.
8. An angel tells Hagar to return and _submit_ to Sarai, for she was to bare a son and call him Ishmael. That he too would be head-strong and many would be against him, but he would dwell in the presence of all his brethren.

9. Hagar calls on God and worships Him.
10. Hagar returns and bares a son, Ismael, to Abram when he was age eighty-six.

Genesis 17:1-14 <u>God makes covenant "**with**" Abram.</u>

1. At the age of ninety-nine, God appears to Abram.
2. Abram falls on his face.
3. God reminds Abram of their last meeting.
4. **God changes his name to Abraham** (Father of Multitudes).
5. God reminds Abraham of the last covenant.
6. God tells Abraham that he must keep that covenant with his heirs.
7. God requires circumcision for all males on the eighth day. This would be a token of that covenant.
8. God warns that all uncircumcised shall be cut off from the covenant inheritance.

Genesis 17:15-19 <u>A blessing for Sarai.</u>

1. **Sarai's name changed to Sarah** (Princess).
2. God would bless her with a son.
3. God tells Sarai she will become a mother of nations.
4. God tells Sarai that Kings would be of her off-spring.
5. Abraham laughed due to his and Sarah's age.
6. Abraham offers his son Ishmael to be his heir, due to Sarah's age of ninety and her inability to conceive in the past.

*GFP: *We should believe God's Word and not depend on our reasoning.*

7. God confirms a son to be born of Sarah and that this child was to be named Isaac.

Genesis 17:20 <u>A blessing for Ishmael.</u>

1. God will bless him.
2. Ishmael will be the father of twelve tribes.
   a. These tribes would become the Arab nations.
   b. These nations claim to be rightful heirs to Abrahamic Covenant.

ABRAHAMIC COVENANT

Genesis 17:21-27 <u>Abraham's Covenant is Established.</u>

1. With Isaac.
2. *Not with Ishmael.* Because Ishmael was **not** the son of Abraham's wife.
3. Abraham confirms the covenant through circumcision of himself and all men of his household.

Genesis 18:1-15 <u>Confirmation due to obedience.</u>

1. Three men come to tell Abraham and Sarah they were about to have a child.
2. Sarah laughs inwardly, knowing she was past the years of child-bearing.
3. God asked if anything was too hard for Him to do.
4. God declares a son would be born.

Genesis 18:16-33 <u>The warning of the loss of Lot.</u>

1. Three men leave and head toward Sodom.
2. God tells Abraham he is about to destroy the cities of Sodom and Gomorrah due to their wickedness.
3. Abraham knew that his nephew Lot lived somewhere in Sodom. He has a dialogue with God hoping to spare his nephew. God says he will not destroy Sodom if there were just ten good men there.

*GFP: *We should always be concerned with the plight of those we love. We should do all we can to warn all of God's judgment upon evil.*

Genesis 19:1-29 <u>The rescue of Lot from Sodom.</u>

1. God sends two angels.
2. Lot met them at the gate of the city.
3. Important men watched at the gate.
4. Lot pressed them to stay at his home.

5. Homosexual men of the city sought to do evil to these visitors.
6. Lot asked them not to do their wickedness.
7. Lot offers them his two virgin daughters instead.
8. The angels intervened by blinding the sodomites.
9. The angels tell Lot of the coming destruction of the city.
10. Lot attempts to get the sons-in-law of his other two daughters to leave the city, but they refused.
11. The angels led Lot, his wife, and their two remaining daughters out of the city.
12. They told them not to look back, lest they be consumed.
13. Lot requested that the angel's take them to a little city nearby named Zoar.
14. The next morning God rained hail fire and brimstone upon Sodom and Gomorah. Nothing was left.
15. Lot's wife looked back and was turned into a pillar like salt by the Dead Sea.
16. Abraham sees the destruction from the other side of the Jordan River.

*GFP: *People do pay for their decisions if they do not obey God's warnings. This does not make God a tyrant. If we choose to break any natural law we suffer the consequences: fire/burn, water/drown, sharp/cut and cold/freeze. We have no one to blame but ourselves.*

Genesis 19:30-38 <u>The Sin of Lot's daughters.</u>

1. Lot's daughters desired their off-spring inherit all Lot had.
2. They got their father drunk and had sex with him to preserve their father's line.
3. Lot did not know this incest had occurred until after the fact.
4. The sons of this incestuous relationship turned out to be the progenitors of the Moabites and Ammonites.

*GFP: *Don't take things into your own hands until you get all the information God will give. The result can be disastrous.*

Genesis 20:1-18 <u>Abraham lies out of fear again.</u>

1. Abraham journeys south to the land of the Philistines.
2. King Abimelech takes Sarah.
3. God warns Abimelech that Sarah is married.

4. Abimelech tells God that he did not lay with her and that he should not be slain.

5. God said he had kept him from Sarah.

6. God told him to restore Sarah to Abraham and he and his people would not die.

7. Abraham tells Abimelech that Sarah "was" his sister. She was the daughter of his father by another mother.
   This is still allowed in some cultures.

8. Abimelech gives Abraham and Sarah gifts and tells them they can live in the land. He also warns everyone to leave them alone.

9. God opens the wombs of the house of Abimelech.

Genesis 21:1-14 <u>Sarah bares the appointed son.</u>

1. Sarah's laughter turned to joy.
2. Sarah's joy turns to bitterness.
3. Sarah asked that Hagar and Ishmael be sent away.
4. Abraham wrestles with a decision.
5. God tells Abraham that everything will be fine.
6. Abraham sees Hagar and Ishmael off.

Genesis 21:15-21 <u>Promise to Hagar fulfilled.</u>

1. Hagar takes Ismael, now fifteen years old, away.
2. They travel toward Egypt.
3. They run out of water.
4. Hagar thinks they are going to die.
5. She goes a short distance away in order that she does not see Ishmael die.
6. God speaks to her from heaven and shows her a well.
7. God tells her not to fear.

*GFP: *God will not allow anyone who follows His principles to go un-rewarded. This is an earthly gift. This does not make that person a God-follower. Remember, a God-follower is one who has accepted God's eternal plan for these teachings: death, burial, burial and resurrection of every God-follower in the future.*

8. Ishmael becomes an archer.
9. Hagar and Ishmael live in Paran.
10. Hagar finds Ishmael an Egyptian wife.

Genesis 21:22-34 <u>A league between Abraham and Abimelech.</u>

1. Abraham stays in the land of the Philistines a long time.

*GFP: *People usually define relationships by what they see in our actions and re-actions.*

Genesis 22:1-19 <u>God tests Abraham's Faith.</u>

1. God **tells** Abraham how to make his son Isaac a witness.
2. Abraham journeys three days to Mt. Moriah.
   (*Today Jerusalem Temple Mount*)
3. Abraham tells the men with him to wait and he and the lad would return. <u>(Abraham believed God would resurrect his son)</u>.
4. Fire in Abraham's hand was flint-stone.
5. Isaac asked about the sacrifice.
6. Abraham tells Isaac that God would provide a lamb for the sacrifice. (God requires the blood of a lamb).
7. Abraham builds and takes out his knife to slay Isaac.
8. An angel calls out to Abraham telling him that because of his obedience, his son was to be spared.
9. Abraham sees a ram caught in bushes.
10. Abraham praises God, and names the place Jehovah-Jireh "God will show you the way".
11. The angel speaks again and verifies the covenant once again to Abraham.

*GFP: *God continually confirms his promises to all who will obey and follow.*

12. Abraham, Isaac and the men return.

Genesis 22:20-24 <u>Record of Abraham's brother Nahor's Eight Sons by Milcah.</u>

1. Nahor has four more sons by his concubine Reumah.
2. *There is also mention of grand-daughter **Rebekah** by Bethuel.

Burying Place for the Seed of Abraham

Genesis 23: <u>Sarah dies at Kir-jath-arbah</u> (Hebron).

1. Sarah dies at one hundred twenty-seven years old.
2. Abraham seeks to purchase burial land from Ephron a Hittite.
3. There was a cave called Mach-pe-lah.
4. Ephron sought to give it to Abraham.
5. Abraham refused.
6. Ephron sold it to him for four hundred shekels of silver.
7. Abraham buries Sarah there.

Genesis 24:1-67 <u>Abraham seeks a bride for his son Isaac.</u>

1. At a late stage in life, Abraham asked his servant Eleazer to seek out of Isaac's kindred, a wife for him.
2. This oath was by putting a hand under a thigh.
3. Abraham sent Eleazer to the city of Nahor, his brother.
4. Eleazer was loaded with gifts.
5. Eleazer stopped and prayed by a well of water prior to entering the city of Nahor.
6. He prayed that the young woman that he sought might come to the well and offer he and his camels water to drink.
7. God answered his prayer immediately.
8. At that moment, Rebekah comes to the well.
9. Eleazer gave her a golden earring and two bracelets of gold, and asked her whose daughter she was.
10. She told him she was the daughter of Bethuel and grand-daughter of Nahor.
11. She told Eleazer that he could lodge at their home.
12. Eleazer bows his head and worships God.
13. Rebekah runs home to tell the head of the house. This was her brother Laban because her grandfather, Nahor and her father, Terah had died.
14. Laban welcomes Eleazer in for a meal.
15. Eleazer told why he was sent.
16. Laban agreed that their meeting was of God.

17. Eleazer bows and worships God again.
18. Eleazer brings in the gifts from Abraham.
19. Rebekah's mother and brother asked if she could stay home at least ten days.
20. Eleazer said he must get back.
21. The mother and Laban said that it is up to Rebekah, thinking she would want to stay.
22. Rebekah said she would go immediately.
23. Eleazer, Rebekah and her handmaid leave after receiving a blessing.
24. Isaac was meditating in a field when he saw the caravan coming.
25. When Rebekah asked who the man was and Eleazer told her it was her betrothed, she jumped off her camel, put on her veil and prepared to meet her future husband.
26. Isaac took her home, married her and was comforted of his mother's death.

Genesis 25:1-4 <u>Abraham's Second wife and family.</u>

1. Abraham's new wife was named Keturah.
2. Keturah bore six sons.
3. These sons bore seven grandsons and three great-grandsons.
4. These sons become bitter enemies of Israel. especially the Midianites.

ABRAHAM'S DEATH

Genesis 25:5-11 <u>Abraham's heritage.</u>

1. Abraham's land and possessions were to go to Isaac.
2. Abraham's other children were given gifts.
3. Abraham's other children were sent out of the land.
4. Abraham dies at age one hundred and seventy- five.
5. Ishmael comes from Paran to help Issac bury Abraham in a sepulcher next to Sarah at Hebron.

*GFP *It often takes a death in a family to allow relatives to see each other. People never forget your presence, time or concern in a time of sorrow or need.*

ISHMAEL'S DESCENDANTS

Genesis 25:12-18 <u>The sons of Ishmael.</u>

1. Ishamel's twelve sons to become twelve nations.
2. Ishmael dies at age one hundred and thirty- seven.
3. All his sons were at his death-bed.

*GFP: *The twelve nations derived from Ishmael are the Arab nations that are enemies with the Nation of Israel today. They will also be among the nations who will descend upon Israel in the Battle of Armageddon mentioned in the prophetic book of Revelation. Many of ISIS fighters are from Ishmael's lineage.*

THE LIFE OF ISAAC
2 FAITH FOLLOWER PATRIARCH

Genesis 25:19-34 <u>Isaac marries Rebekah at age forty.</u>

1. Rebekah was from Syria.
2. Rebekah was barren.
3. Isaac prayed to the Lord twenty years.
4. Rebekah had twins.
5. God told Rebekah that these two boys would rule two nations.
6. God told Rebekah her first born would serve the younger.
7. When the sons were born the first was red haired and hairy all over. The second son was holding onto the heel of the first.
8. Isaac and Rebekah named the boys Esau and Jacob.
9. Isaac was sixty years old when they were born.
10. Esau grew up to be a hunter. Jacob grew up staying close to home.
11. Isaac favored Esau. Rebekah favored Jacob.

*GFP: *Never favor one child over the other! Yes, they may have qualities you admire more, and you should let those be known, but always express your love and appreciation for each child. Do this both privately and publicly. Children know they are different and want to be recognized for their individual characteristics.*

12. One day Esau had been working in the fields and said he was about to starve. Jacob said, if you are so hungry sell me your birthright by swearing to me.
13. Esau swore to Jacob.
14. From that day forth, Esau despised his birthright.

Genesis 26:1-33 <u>A Famine in the Land.</u>

1. Isaac did as his father and went to King Abimelech the Philistine.
2. Isaac was about to go down to Egypt when God appeared to him.
3. God reminded Isaac of the covenant he made with his father, Abraham.

4. Isaac remained in Gerar, but lied about Rebekah.

*GFP: *Many of our children are just becoming followers of the examples they see.*

5. King Abimelech, still having his woman problem, saw Isaac fondling Rebekah during play. He then knew that she was not his sister.
6. Abimelech warns his people of this lie and possibility of judgment for touching her.

*GFP: *We are to warn others of possible judgment for improper living. It is the same as knowing a bridge is out, a tornado is coming or electrical wires are down. With knowledge comes responsibility.*

7. Isaac continued to multiply and became very wealthy.
8. Therefore, King Abimelech asked Isaac to leave the land.
9. Isaac moved to the valleys and re-digged the wells of his father Abraham.
10. The Philistines claimed all the wells that Isaac digged. Isaac moved to Beer-sheba.
11. God appeared to Isaac in a dream, once again, reminding him of his blessing through his father, Abraham.
12. Isaac built an altar at Beer-sheba and digged a well.
13. Abimelech saw the blessing of God on Isaac and came to him asking that he make a league with the Philistines to do them no harm. Isaac agrees.
14. The seventh well that Isaac's men dug had plenty of water. Isaac called it the place of the seventh well, Beer-sheba.

Genesis 26:34-35 Joy turns to sorrow.

1. At age forty, Esau marries two wives of the pagan Hittites.
2. This is another reason Esau lost his birthright.
3. Isaac and Rebekah grieved over the actions of their son, Esau.

Genesis 27:1- Rebekah is willing to be cursed

1. Isaac about to die.
2. Isaac could not see well (glaucoma).
3. Isaac wanted to bless Esau.
4. Isaac sends Esau to kill a deer and make him some soup that he loves.

5. Rebekah overhears Isaac's conversation.
6. Rebekah tells Jacob that he was about to lose the son's blessing and that he should obey her.
7. Jacob tells his mother that his father will know that he is not Esau because Esau was a hairy man. That Isaac will feel him and curse him for his deceit.
8. Rebekah tells Jacob that he should obey her and she would take the curse.
9. Rebekah took the clothes of Esau and put them on Jacob. She put the skins of goats upon his hands and neck. She made the soup and sent Jacob to his father.

*GFP: *Rebekah's actions were just another of the methods that lead to a family's destruction.*

10. Isaac was tricked and blessed Jacob.
11. About the end of Jacob's blessing Esau came in with soup.
12. Esau weeps bitterly and asked that his father bless him also.
13. Isaac told Esau that he had been tricked, and the blessing had gone to Jacob.
14. Esau begs for a blessing.
15. Isaac told Esau that he would live off the fatness of the earth and he would have to battle his way to greatness. Then after many years he would break the bondage of Jacob's yoke.

*GFP: *Solutions don't just come, they must be found.*

16. For the loss of his birthright and blessing, Esau despised Jacob.
17. Esau planned to kill Jacob after Isaac dies.
18. Rebekah hears of Esau's death-wish and and tells Jacob to flee to her brother, Laban in Haran, until Esau gets over his anger.
19. Rebekah tells Isaac that she is scared that Jacob will marry a wife from the idol worshipers of Heth as did Esau. Then there would be no lineage of God followers.

Notes

THE LIFE OF JACOB
3 FAITH FOLLOWER PATRIARCH

Genesis 28:1-22 <u>Jacob flees for his life.</u>

1. Isaac charges Jacob not to marry a Canaanite.
2. Isaac tells Jacob to go north to the house of Laban, and find a wife there.
3. Isaac passes on to Jacob the covenant of Abraham.
4. Esau out of spite marries Ishmael's daughter. (Joins the Arab nations).
5. Jacob has a dream of a ladder reaching up to heaven. God confirms the Abrahamic Covenant with him. Jacob realizes this is a special place and names this place Beth- el, the dwelling place of God.
6. Jacob vowed to God that **if** God would be with him and do all that he said, **then** he would serve God.
7. Jacob promises to give God a tenth (tithe) of all that God blessed him with.

Genesis 29:1-35 <u>Jacob arrives in Haran.</u>

1. Jacob meets up with men watering their flocks at a well.
2. Jacob questions if they know Laban and his welfare. They responded yes! he was doing fine.
3. While they spoke, Rachel, a daughter of Laban, comes to water sheep.
4. Jacob went near and rolled the stone from the wells mouth and began watering the flock of Laban.
5. He then greeted Rachel with a family kiss and told her he was kin. That his mother was Rebekah, Laban's sister.
6. Rachel ran home to tell her brother Laban.
7. Laban runs to greet Jacob to find out the welfare of his sister.
8. Laban kissed him and brought him home.
9. Jacob stays for a month serving Laban.
10. Laban tells Jacob that he should not work without wages. Laban asked Jacob what would he work for.

11. Jacob tells Laban he would work seven years for the hand of Rachel his youngest daughter.

12. Laban agrees.

13. Jacob works seven years and plans his wedding.

14. On the night of the wedding Laban sneaks his oldest daughter Leah into the marriage tent. A marriage of deception.

15. Jacob is not aware of the trick until the light of day.

16. Jacob asked why he had tricked him.

17. Laban said it was unlawful in his land to marry a younger daughter before an elder daughter.

18. Laban tells Jacob to work seven years for Rachel and she could be his wife.

19. Jacob worked another seven years for Rachel.

20. Jacob loved Rachel more than Leah.

21. Rachel was barren.

22. Leah conceived and bare a son **Reuben**. She thought Jacob would surely love her now.

23. Leah conceived again and bare a son **Simeon**. She bore a third son **Levi**. And then a fourth son **Judah** and bare no more children.

Genesis 30:1-37 <u>Rachel has a plan.</u>

1. Leah has a handmaid Zilpah and Rachel has a handmaid Bilhah.

2. Out of jealousy Rachel told Jacob that he had to give her sons or she would die.

*GFP: *We often exaggerate our circumstances to allow us to create the conditions that would be more desirable.*

3. Jacob says he is not God.

4. Rachel then tells Jacob to impregnate Bilhah and she would raise that child as her own.

5. Bilhah has a son **Dan**, then a second son **Naphtali**.

6. Leah is jealous and gives Zilpah to Jacob.

7. Zilpah bares a son **Gad**, then a second son **Asher**.

8. Rachel trades a night with Jacob for some mandrakes, which are edible plants, and Leah has a fifth son **Issachar** and a sixth son **Zebulun**.

9. Leah bares a daughter Dinah. Leah has now born seven children, **out of devotion,** to Jacob.

10. God opens Rachel's womb and she bares a son **Joseph**.

11. Now after twenty-one years, Jacob has the rightful heir.

Notes

12. Jacob asked Laban to grant him his wages that he may return to his homeland with his family.

13. Laban asked Jacob to stay because he knows how God blessed him because of Jacob.

14. Jacob tells Laban that he does not have to give him anything, but allow him to go a little distance and separate the few speckled and spotted cattle for himself. That in the future any solid animals shall be Laban's and the speckled and spotted ones Jacobs.

15. Laban agrees and has his sons separate the cattle a three days journey.

16. Jacob takes branches of popular, hazelnut and chestnut trees and peeled sections of the bark till the white appeared.

17. He set the rods before the face of the healthier cattle and when they conceived they bare mixed colored offspring.

18. He did not put the rods before the weaker and they bare solid, which were Laban's. *This is the first mention of Selective Breeding.*

19. Jacob's herds increase until the sons of Laban claimed that Jacob has stolen what was their fathers.

20. Jacob also realized that Laban did not treat him as before.

21. Jacob warns Rachel and Leah of their father's change of heart and of his past deceits in the past.

22. Jacob's wives agree that what they have has been granted of God. And that whatsoever God has told Jacob to do, do it.

Genesis 31:17-55 Jacob has a plan.

1. Jacob gets ready to go back to the land of Canaan without telling Laban.

2. Rachel had stolen Laban's Syrian idols.

3. Laban hears about this and gets his brethren and pursues after Jacob.

4. God warned Laban in a dream and told him to speak neither good or bad to Jacob.

5. Laban and his men catch Jacob and his family camped at Mt. Gilead.

6. Laban pitches his tents also at Mt. Gilead and asked Jacob why he stole away his daughters as captives. Laban said he would have seen them off with joy.

7. Laban warns that he had the power to hurt them, but that Jacob's God had warned him the night before.

8. Then he accused Jacob of stealing his gods.

9. Jacob explains why he left and says he knows nothing of his gods, but he could search all that he had.

10. Laban searches and finds nothing because Rachel was sitting on them. She asked her father to excuse her for not getting up because she was on her menstrual cycle. Therefore, he did not find them.

11. Jacob is angry and reminds Laban of all his labor and that if God had not warned him, he would have killed him there.

12. Laban asked Jacob to make a covenant between the two.

13. Jacob made a heap of stones and Laban said that these stones would be a witness between the two of them. That this heap would be a boundary. That neither should pass to the other side to do harm to the other.

14. Jacob swore the oath also.

15. The next morning Laban kissed all Jacob's family goodbye and went home.

Genesis 32:1-33:20 <u>Jacob fears Esau from the past.</u>

1. Jacob meets God's host, or angels, while returning home. He names the place Ma-ha-na-im, meaning two camps.

2. Jacob sent ambassadors to Esau in Edom telling him that Jacob was returning home, but he would be a servant to Esau. That he had been in the homeland of his mother for the past twenty-one years. That he had also acquired much wealth.

3. The ambassadors returned saying: Esau was coming to meet him with four hundred men.

4. Jacob cries to God; and admits his un- worthiness for all that God had done for him. Then he asked God to deliver him.

5. Jacob reminds God of his promise to bless him and protect his generations.

6. He lodged there and got together many gifts of cattle, sheep and goats. He told his servants to lead each herd separately with a distance between each herd.

7. He told the leader of the first herd to tell Esau that his herd is a gift from his servant, Jacob. He said the same to the leader of each herd in order to appease Esau prior to seeing him face to face.

8. That night Jacob took his two wives and all his children with all he had across the brook Jabbok.

9. Jacob was left alone.

10. That night Jacob wrestled with an angel and could not win. The angel dislocated Jacob's hip bone as they wrestled. The angel asked Jacob to let him go because it was the breaking of day. Jacob

Notes

would not let him go unless he would give him a blessing. The angel asked him what was his name. He replied: Jacob.

11. The angel said he would no longer be called Jacob, but ISRAEL.

12. Jacob asked the angel his name? The angel said he should know his name. Then the angel blessed him. Jacob then knew it was God. Jacob named the place Pen-i-el.

13. Jacob had a limp from then on. The people of Israel still don't eat the ligaments, joints or the thigh of animals.

Genesis 33:1-15 Jacob meets Esau

1. Jacob sees Esau and four hundred men coming.

2. Jacob puts Zilpah and Bilah and their children in front, then Leah and her children second.

3. Rachel and her children along with Jacob were last.

4. As they drew close to Esau, Jacob bowed down seven times to his brother.

5. Esau ran and embraced Jacob and asked, who are all these people?

6. Jacob tells Esau they are his blessing from God and they are now his servants.

7. Esau said he has enough servants already and that Jacob take some of his.

8. Jacob replies no, and asked permission to continue on to find a home in Canaan.

9. Esau returns to Seir *(Edom)*.

10. Jacob comes to Succoth and builds a house there.

11. Jacob bought land in Shalem *(Jerusalem)* and erected an altar there.

DINAH

The First Woman's Story in the Bible

Genesis 34:1-31 <u>Keeping a promise.</u>

1. Leah's daughter, Dinah, went out among the daughters of non-followers.
2. A prince named Shechem of the Hivites saw her beauty, took her and her virginity.
3. He falls in love with her and seeks to marry her to make things right.
4. Shechem and his father, Hamor, went to Jacob to see if they could arrange the marriage. (this was the custom if a man had sex with a virgin).
5. Hamor also asked if all their sons and daughters could marry.
6. But Jacob's sons heard that their sister had been defiled by other than an Israelite.
7. Jacob's sons responded that they would allow this if all the Hivite men would be as they were; circumcised.
8. Jacob's sons said if they would not do this, they would leave the land with their daughters.
9. All the men of the Hivites agreed thinking all the belongings of Jacob would soon be theirs.
10. Three days after they were circumcised, Leah's sons Simeon and Levi slew all the Hivite males with the sword. They also brought back Dinah and spoiled the city.
11. Jacob tells his sons that what they did had given a bad name to Israel and that they would have to leave that land.

Genesis: 35:1- <u>Jacob flees back to Bethel.</u>

1. Jacob goes to where he first fled from Esau.
2. Jacob told his families to put away any idols, foreign clothing and jewelry they might have.
3. Jacob told the people to purify themselves to worship.

4. Jacob builds an altar to God.
5. Jacob hides all his jewelry under an oak in Shechem.
6. God places fear of them on the surrounding cities and they were able to get away.
7. Deborah, Rebekah's midwife, died and was buried at Bethel.
8. God reminds him of the Abrahamic Covenant.
9. Jacob moves toward his land in Shalem.
10. On the way, Rachel begins birth pains. She feels as though she is going to die and says that the son shall be called Ben-o- ni (son of my sorrow), but Jacob called his name **Benjamin** (son of my right hand).
11. Rachel dies giving birth and was buried on the road to Bethlehem (House of Bread).
12. Reuben commits incest with Jacob's concubine Bilhah.
13. A list of the remainder of Jacob's twelve Sons.
14. Jacob goes to Hebron and his father Isaac dies at age one hundred and eighty.
15. Esau hears and comes to help Jacob bury their father.

THE GENERATIONS OF ESAU

Genesis 36:1-19 <u>The continuation of the Arab Nations.</u>

1. Esau's wives were:
    a. Adah the Hittite.
    b. Aholibamah the Hivite.
    c. Bashemath the daughter of Ishmael.
2. Esau and his families dwelt in southern Jordan, known as Edom.
3. Esau had ten sons.
4. All his sons became Dukes in Edom.

Genesis 36:20-43 <u>Relatives of Esau through marriage.</u>

1. Brother and sister in laws.
2. Kings that reigned in Edom before Israel had a king.
    a. Bela
    b. Jobab
    c. Husham
    d. Hadad
    e. Samlah
    f. Saul (not Israel's first king).
    g. Baalhanan
    h. Hadar

Notes

THE LIFE OF JOSEPH
#4 FAITH FOLLOWER PATRIARCH

Genesis 37:1- <u>Joseph the braggart.</u>

1. Jacob loved Joseph more than all his sons.
2. Jacob made him a coat of many colors, *which* shows heir or royalty.
3. Joseph's brothers despised him.
4. Joseph dreams about his message from God and told his brothers.
5. This causes his brothers to despise him more.
6. Jacob rebuked Joseph for telling the dreams to his brothers.
7. Jacob asked Joseph if even his mother and father would bow down to him in the future.
8. Jacob kept Joseph's sayings in his heart because he remembers how God spoke to him.
9. One day when the brothers were feeding the flocks in Shechem, Joseph was sent by Jacob to check on the welfare of his brothers.
10. He got lost and a man told him that his brothers had gone south to Dothan.
11. Joseph goes and finds them.
12. When his brothers see him coming, they conspired to slay him and throw him into a pit (dried up well).
13. They would say some beast had eaten him.
14. Reuben stopped them from killing him, but cast him into a pit. Reuben planned to come back later to deliver Joseph to his father. The eldest is required to replace blood for blood.
15. They stripped Joseph of his coat and cast him into a pit.
16. Later a caravan of Ishmaelites came by.
17. Judah convinced his brothers not to shed Joseph's blood, but to sell him to the merchants.
18. They sold Joseph for twenty pieces of silver.
19. Joseph was taken to Egypt.
20. The brothers killed a baby goat, took Joseph's coat and smeared the blood on it.
21. They told Jacob that they found it in the way. That Joseph undoubtedly had been eaten by some beast.

22. When Jacob heard the story, he rent his clothes and mourned many days. None of the family could comfort him.

23. The merchants sold Joseph to Potiphar, a captain of the guard of the Pharoah (Amenenhet II) of Egypt.

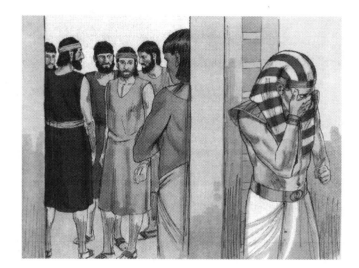

STORY OF JUDAH

Genesis 38:1-30 <u>Judah marries a non-follower.</u>

1. Judah goes to the land of the Adullamites.
2. He marries a Canaanite woman named Shuah.
3. She bares him three sons:
    a. Er, meaning watchful.
    b. Onan, meaning strong.
    c. Shelah, meaning petition.
4. Er was wicked and God cut his life short.
5. Judah told his second son Onan to marry Er's wife Tamar and to conceive a family with her.
6. Onan did not want to do this, so when he had intercourse, he spilled his seed on the ground.
7. God was displeased with Onan and slew him. <u>The Hebrews were to propagate the God- follower line.</u>
8. Judah asked Tamar, his daughter-in-law, to remain a widow until his third son Shelah was able to bare children.
9. Tamar went to live with her father.
10. After a long time, Judah's wife, Shuah, died.
11. Tamar realized that Judah was not going to keep his word; for Shelah was now a young man.
12. Tamar heard that Judah was going to Timnath to shear sheep. She put off her widow's garment and put on a veil and harlot's clothes. She waited along the wayside.
13. When Judah saw her, he asked her what was her price, not knowing it was Tamar.
14. Judah said he would send her a kid goat. Tamar asked that he give her his signet ring as a pledge until she got the goat. Judah went in to her and she conceived.
15. Judah went on his way, but got one of his servants to take a kid goat to her.
16. When the servant got to the place, she was gone. The local men said: We know of no harlot here.
17. Three months later Judah found out that Tamar was pregnant.

18. Judah sent for Tamar and asked what man she had been with.
19. She showed him his signet ring, bracelets and staff he had left behind in his rush not to be seen with a harlot.
20. Judah acknowledged his belongings and told Tamar that she was more righteous than him.
21. Tamar had twins.
22. During birth a baby reached out its hand. The midwife put a scarlet thread around its wrist. It drew its hand back into the womb. Upon the first delivery, it was a boy, but no thread upon his hand. His name was Pharez or breach born.
23. Afterward the baby with the scarlet thread upon his wrist came and was named Zerah or dawn.

*GFP: *Tamar is found in the lineage of the Tribe of Judah and in the lineage of Jesus the Christ of the New Testament. This lets us know God is no respecter of persons. He is willing to forgive any sin. This story also shows He can use any of us to accomplish His divine plan.*

Notes

JOSEPH IN EGYPT

Genesis 39-41 <u>God makes Joseph prosper.</u>

1. His master Potiphar saw that God was with him.
2. God blessed Potiphar's house because of Joseph.

*GFP: *God often blesses others for helping his Followers.*

3. He gave Joseph rule over all that he had and Potiphar did not know what he had.
4. Joseph was a good person and very nice looking.
5. After some time, Potiphar's wife was attracted to him. She propositioned Joseph, but he refused.
6. Joseph told her he could not betray someone who had made him greater than anyone in his household; and he would not sin against God.

*GFP: *Notice Joseph did not say he could not sin against God. We all can sin at any time. Joseph was so committed that he would not betray his God.*

7. Potiphar's wife continued to pursue Joseph.
8. One day Joseph came into the house to use the bathroom. No one else was in the house and she caught him by his robe asking him to lie with her.
9. Joseph fled leaving his robe.
10. She called for the servants and said that this Hebrew shepherd was mocking them. That he tried to seduce her. She then said she screamed and Joseph fled. Then she showed the servants his robe.
11. She waited to tell the story to Potiphar.
12. Potiphar was so mad that he threw Joseph into prison.
13. God was with Joseph in the prison.
14. Joseph was made a trustee over all the prisoners.

Genesis 40:1-23 <u>Joseph puts dreams to good use.</u>

1. The Kings butler and baker were also placed in prison.
2. Joseph was over them.
3. Each of the men dreamed a dream.
4. Joseph told them that God helped him interpret dreams.
5. The butler told him his dream
6. Joseph told the butler that he would be restored to his position in three days.
7. Joseph told him to mention him to the Pharoah, Amenenhet II.
8. The baker wanted Joseph to interpret his dream for good also.
9. But Joseph told the baker that he would be hanged in three days.
10. In three days, on Pharoah's birthday, he restored the butler and hanged the baker.
11. The chief butler forgot Joseph's plea.

Genesis 41:1-43 <u>Joseph interprets Pharoah's dream.</u>

1. Two years later the Pharoah dreamed a dream of seven fat cows and seven skinny cows.
2. He dreamed a second dreamed of seven ears of good corn and seven ears of thin corn.
3. None of the magicians of Egypt could tell the Pharoah the meaning of his dream.
4. The butler then remembered the promise he had made Joseph. He told the Pharoah the account of his dream and that the Hebrew Joseph could interpret the dream with his God's help.
5. Joseph comes to the Pharoah and interprets his two dreams as one. There would be seven good years followed by seven years of famine.
6. Joseph told the Pharoah to seek a man wise enough to save the land.
7. The Pharoah said that since Joseph was wise enough to know the dream, he would be wise enough to know how to take care of the land.
8. The Pharoah set Joseph over all the land of Egypt. He placed his signet on Joseph's hand and told him that there would be none greater than him in Egypt.
9. The Pharoah changes his name to Zaph-nath-pa-a-ne-ah, and gave him, Asenath, the daughter of Potipherah, priest of On, in marriage.

Genesis 41:46-57 <u>Joseph begins to rule over all Egypt.</u>

1. Joseph was thirty years old when he began to rule Egypt.
2. During the seven good years Joseph builds barns to hold the plenteous harvest.
3. All the surrounding countries came to Joseph during the seven years of famine.
4. Joseph and Asenath had two sons, Manasseh and Ephraim, during the seven years of plenty.

JACOB SENDS HIS 10 SONS TO EGYPT

Genesis 42:1-38 <u>The famine affects Jacob's tribes.</u>

1. Jacob sent all his sons except Benjamin to Egypt.
2. Jacob was afraid of losing his only heir.
3. Jacob's ten sons entered Egypt to purchase corn.
4. They had to purchase that corn from Joseph.
5. They did not recognize Joseph.
6. Joseph did recognize them, but spoke through an interpreter.
7. Joseph accused them of being spies.
8. Jacob's sons tell Joseph that they are ten of twelve brothers from the land of Canaan.
9. Joseph tells them to prove they are not spies by one of them retrieving the youngest brother. The remaining brothers would remain in jail until all the brothers were in Egypt.
10. The brothers all agreed that they were in this plight because of what they had done to Joseph.
11. Joseph heard their grief and had to leave from their presence to weep.
12. Joseph changed his mind, placed Simeon only in jail, loads the other brother's sacks with corn and food for the three days return journey.
13. Joseph also hid each brother's payment in the top of their sacks.
14. When each brother emptied their sacks in the presence of their father, Jacob declared that they had now bereaved all his tribe. That Joseph was gone, Simeon was gone and now he was about to lose Benjamin.
15. Reuben told Jacob that he may kill his two sons if he does not bring Benjamin back.
16. Jacob refuses to send Benjamin and considers Simeon dead also. Jacob counts his loses and attempts to live on what his sons had brought back.

Notes

Genesis 43:1-34 <u>A greater famine changes Jacob's heart.</u>

1. Jacob, now known as Israel, *man of God,* told his sons to return to Egypt to buy more corn.
2. Israel's sons refuse unless their father sends Benjamin with them.
3. Judah told his father that he would place his life in his father's hand if he did not return with Benjamin.
4. Israel gives in, but told his sons to also take gifts to the man and return the money they returned with on the first trip.
5. When the brothers returned, and stood before Joseph, he had the men brought to his home.
6. Israel's sons feared for their lives and explained to Joseph's steward what had taken place.
7. The steward told them not to fear, for their God, and the God of their father had spared them.
8. The steward brought Simeon, then had them clean up for a noon meal with Joseph.
9. When Joseph came home his brothers gave him the gifts of Israel and they bowed themselves before Joseph.
10. Joseph asked if Israel was still alive.
11. The brothers replied yes and bowed again.
12. Joseph then sees Benjamin, <u>his mother</u> <u>Rachel's son.</u>
13. Joseph leaves the room to weep alone.
14. Joseph washes his face and returns to eat.
15. Joseph sat at his own table as it was not proper for an Egyptian to eat with Hebrews.
16. Joseph saw to it that each of his brothers had plenty to eat. But Benjamin received 5 times as much the food as his brothers.

Genesis 44:1-34 <u>Joseph's new plan.</u>

1. Joseph has his brothers stay the night.
2. He told his steward to fill and return the payment in their sacks again and also put his personal silver cup in one of the sacks.
3. Joseph's brothers left the next morning at daylight.
4. After a short time, Joseph told his steward to go after them and accuse them of stealing his cup that he drinks from to interpret the future.
5. Joseph's brothers remind the steward of their honesty in the past. They tell him to search their sacks; and if he finds the cup among them, that man may be killed.
6. The cup was found in Benjamin's sack.

7. The brothers tore their clothes in sorrow and went back to Joseph's house and asked how they could clear their names.

8. Joseph told them that the man whose sack contained the cup would be his servant.

9. Joseph declares that the other brothers could go home.

10. Judah asked to speak to Joseph privately. Judah explains that Benjamin is the only heir of his father who is old and feeble.

11. Judah tells the story of Joseph and how it sorrowed Israel.

12. He then tells that he had given his life for a surety; but that if he does not bring back Benjamin his father would die.

Genesis 45:1-47:10 Joseph explains his prosperity.

1. Joseph burst into tears and cried loudly asking the room to be cleared with the exception of his brothers.

2. Joseph revealed himself and told his brothers how God had sent him to Egypt to preserve them.

3. Joseph told them that there is still five years of famine to come. They must go and get Israel.

4. Joseph told them the Hebrews shall dwell in the land of Goshen, the Gaza Strip.

5. All Egypt heard of Joseph and his brothers.

6. The Pharoah also sent for Israel and the Hebrews.

7. God told Israel to go to Egypt and that he would bring them back one day.

8. Israel and sixty-six family members were brought to Egypt. Add Joseph, his wife and two sons, and the total number of Hebrews would be seventy.

9. Joseph told the Pharoah that his family are shepherds. *Shepherds are the lowest of life to the Egyptians*. The Pharoah agrees to let the Hebrews stay in Goshen.

10. Israel told the Pharoah he was one hundred and thirty years old, and he blessed Pharoah and went on his way.

Genesis 47:11-26 Joseph makes the Pharoah supreme.

1. In the third through the seventh years of the famine Joseph exchanged grain for money, then cattle, then land. That made the people servants of Pharoah.

2. Joseph made a law that everyone, except the priest, would give twenty percent (20%) of all that they had to the Pharoah. The people were glad to do so, for Joseph had saved their lives.

Notes

*GFP: *God-followers give out of thanks and obedience, not because of fear or pressure. They believe God is moving people to make all happen for their good. Therefore, all they have is because of God.*

Genesis 47:27-49:33 <u>Israel blesses his sons and dies.</u>

1. Israel lived in Egypt for seventeen years He was one hundred and forty-seven years old. He made his sons swear that he would be buried in Hebron with his ancestors.

*GFP: *Jacob wanted to be buried with Leah, not Rachel. Jacob had possibly grown to love Leah for her faithfulness. Love grows through trust and faithfulness. Lust grows through sexual desire and selfishness. Love becomes stronger while lust becomes a weakness.*

2. Joseph learns his father Israel is about to die. Joseph comes with his two sons to Israel.
3. Israel blesses Joseph's sons, knowingly blessing Ephraim, the younger, first. He then blessed Manasseh.
4. Israel told Joseph that he would return to Canaan. He gave Joseph a double portion of land.
5. Israel blesses his other sons.
6. Israel dies.

Genesis 50:1-13 <u>Israel(Jacob) embalmed and carried to Hebron.</u>

1. The Egyptian embalming process of forty days takes place for the first Hebrew.
2. Joseph seeks permission to take his father to Hebron.
3. The Pharoah told Joseph to obey the oath to Israel. All the servants and elders of the Pharoah, and all Israel's family less the small children were sent to mourn Israel.
4. Before crossing the Jordan River, the company camped and mourned seven days.
5. When the inhabitants of the surrounding areas saw the mourning they were astounded and assumed this was a great Egyptian or a mighty man.
6. Israel was placed in the tomb at Hebron.

Genesis 50:14-26 <u>Joseph's brothers now afraid of</u> <u>Retribution.</u>

1. Joseph returns to Egypt with his family.
2. Joseph's brothers send a message to him saying that Israel had asked that Joseph forgive them of their evil they had done to him.
3. When they appeared before Joseph he wept as they spoke to him. They fell down before Joseph and declared they would be his servants.
4. Joseph told them even though they thought evil against him, God turned it to good.
5. Joseph also told them he was where God wanted him and he would be good to them and their children.
6. Joseph lived long enough to see his children to the third generation.
7. He told his family that God would lead them out of Egypt to the land of promise of Abraham, Isaac and Jacob.
8. Joseph made his family swear they would carry his bones when they departed from Egypt.
9. Joseph died being one hundred and ten years old. He was embalmed and placed in a coffin in Egypt. Amenenhet III was the ruling pharaoh at Joseph's death.

Appendix

As a student of biblical studies you should use every available and reliable source to confirm names, locations, lineage, histories and backgrounds.

Some helpful sites and helps are:

1. Ancient biblical maps.
2. BiblePlaces.com
3. Bible maps and charts.
4. Rose Publishing.
5. www.bible.ca
6. Israel My Glory magazine.
7. The Great Courses
8. Encyclopedia of the Bible
9. Who's Who in the Bible
10. Handbook of Biblical Chronology

The Months of the year as named by Adam

1st month **Abib** or **Nissan** = April
2nd month **Zif** = May
3rd month **Sivan** = June
4th month **Tammuz** = July
5th month **Ab** = August
6th month **Elul** = September
7th month **Ethamin** = October
8th month **Bul** = November
9th month **Chisleu** = December
10th month **Tabeth** = January
11th month **Sebat** = Feburary
12th month **Adar** = March

The first day of each month is called the new moon. The Ancient Calendar contained 360 days to a year. Each seventh year would have an extra month, which was the month of rest for the land and people. Every 49 years would have an extra year, which was the year of Jubilee. In this year all debts were forgiven and lost land was returned to the original family owners.

Old Testament Locations of Today

Accad = Babylonian city of Nimrod

Ammon = Jordanian city of Amman

Ar = Capital of Moab

Aram = Syria (Armenia)

Arphaxad = Ur (Southern Euphrates)

Ashdod = Philistine Seacoast city

Askelon = Philistine Seacoast city

Ashkenaz = Scythians (Russia)

Ashtaroth = Jordanian city

Asshur = Mesopotamia (Assyria)

Babel = Mesopotamia (Sumer, Shinar)

Babyalon = Iraq

Beersheba = Southern Israel

Bethlehem = 5 miles S/W from Jerusalem

Bethel = 12 miles N from Jerusalem

Canaan = Land of Syria and Palestine

Calah = Nimrud in Iraq

Chaldea = Southern Babylon (Iraq)

Charchemish = Northern Euphrates

Cush = Africa

Damascus = Capital of Syria

Dor = Canaanite town of Manasseh

Dothan = Near the Sothern Tip of the Sea of Galilee

Eden = Fork of Tigris/Euphrates city

Elam = Persia

Gaza = Gaza Strip

Gerar = Between Gaza and Beersheba

Gomer = Northern Turkey

Goshen = North Eastern Egypt

Hamath = Hama, Syria

Haran = Southeast Turkey (Balikh)

Hebron = Kiriath-arba in Israel

Hittites = Central Turkey

Javan = Greece

Joppa = Modern Tel Aviv Israel

Jerusalem = Ancient Capital of Israel

Joktan = Arabia

Kadesh-Barnea = Oasis S of Beer-sheba

Kittim = Cyprus

Lud = Lydia in Turkey

Madai = Medes (Iran)

Mamre = City near Hebron in S Israel

Mari = Centrally located on Euphrates River

Midan = East of Gulf of Aqaba

Mizram = Egypt

Moab = S/E land of the Dead Sea

Mt. Ararat = Turkey

Nuzu =

Padan-aram = N Mesopotamia (Syria)

Philistia = Southern Israel

Rameses = Capital City of Egypt and store city

Pithom = East of Nile delta (ancient store city)

Put = North Western Egypt

Sinai = Peninsula separating the Red Sea

Seir = Another name for Elam

Shechem = Near Mt. Gerizim in Israel

Shittim = Plains of Moab

Shur = N/W part of Sinai Peninsula

Siddim = Southern end of Dead Sea

Sidon = Phoenician port of Lebanon

Succoth = Jordan Valley

Tyre = Phoenician Port in Lebanon

Togarmah =

Ur = Southern Babylonia (Iraq)

Uz = Edom in Arabia

Zeboiim = One of 5 cites linked with
        Sodom and Gomorah

Simple List of Biblical Historical Books, Events and Characters

Genesis 1-11   Creation   **(In the land of Mesopotamia)**
                    Fall
                    Flood
                    Tower of Babel

Genesis 12-50

                    Abraham   **(In the land of Canaan and Egypt)**
                    Isaac
                    Jacob (Israel)
                    Joseph

Exodus

Leviticus   Moses   **(In the land of Egypt)**
Numbers   **Exodus 1446BC according**
Deuteronomy   **to Ezra**

Joshua   Joshua   **(In the land of Canaan)**
                    Caleb
Judges   Othniel
                    Ehud
                    Shamgar
                    Deborah and Barak
                    Gideon
                    Abimelech
                    Tola
                    Jair
                    Jephthah
                    Ibsan
                    Elon
                    Abdon
                    Samson
                    Eli
                    Samuel

Ruth	Ruth	*(In land of Moab and Israel)*
	Naomi	
	Boaz	
I Samuel	Samuel	
II Samuel	Saul	**(United Kingdom/Saul to Solomon)**
I Kings	David	
II Kings	Solomon	
I Chronicles	Elijah	**(Prophet to Nation of Israel)**
II Chronicles	Elias	**(Prophet to People of Israel)**

The Divided Kingdom

1. ISRAEL is called the Northern Kingdom.
   a. Its capital is Samaria.
   b. It had 19 wicked kings.
   c. ISRAEL was captured by Assyria for good 722 B.C.

2. JUDAH is called the Southern Kingdom and
   a. Its capital is Jerusalem.
   b. It had 7 good and 12 bad kings.
   c. JUDAH was captured by Babylon for 70 yrs. in 586 B.C.

Ezra	**(In the land of Persia)**
Nehemiah	**(In the land of Shushan)**
Esther	**(In the land of Shushan)**
Job	*(In land of Uz)* (Oldest book of Bible)
Psalms	Writings of David, Natan, Asaph, Ethan and Moses.
Proverbs	Writings of Solomon.
Ecclesiastes	(son of King David)
Song of Solomon	

Isaiah	Prophet during the reigns of Uzziah, Jotham, Ahaz, Hezekiah and all the kings of Judah.
Jeremiah	Priest of Anathoth in the reign of Josiah
Lamentations	King of Judah.
Ezekiel	Prophet during the reign of Jehoiachin King of Israel.
Daniel	Prophet in Babylon during the captivity of Nebuchadnezzar.

Hosea	Prophet during the reigns of Uzziah, Jotham, Ahaz and Hezekiah kings of Judah.
Joel	Prophet to Zion and the nation of Judah.
Amos	Prophet to Judah and Israel during the reigns of Uzziah of Judah and Jeroboam of Israel.
Obadiah	Prophet to Edom and captivity of Israel.
Jonah	Prophet to warn Nineveh.
Micah	Prophet during the reigns of Jotham, Ahaz and Hezekiah kings of Judah.
Nahum	Prophet against Nineveh.
Habakkuk	Prayer for Shigionoth.
Zephaniah	Prophet to Judah.
Haggai	Prophet for Zerubbabel, the governor, and Joshua the high priest in Media.
Zechariah	Prophet to Darius, King of the Medes and Persians.
Malachi	Prophet to warn Israel.

Summary of Leaders of Captivities During the Divided Kingdom of Israel

Assyria 722-612 B.C.   **(never returned as a tribe)**

Tiglath Pileser III
Shalmanezar V
Sargon II
Sennacherib
Esarhaddon
Asurbanipal

Babylon 612-539 B.C.   **(70 yr. captivity and returned as kingdom of Judah)**

Nebuchadnezzar
Nabonidus

Persia 539-331 B.C.   **(returns led by Ezra and Zerubbabel)**

Belshazzar
Cyrus II
Cambees II
Darius I
Xerxes I (Ahasuerus)
Artaxerxes

A BIBLICAL TIMELINE

Note: These dates are from the author's dating and are approximate to plus or minus 10 years up to Moses birth.

From Adam to Noah 3766-2709= 1056 B.C.
From Noah to Flood 1056-1656 B.C.
From Flood to Joseph 1656-1938 B.C
450(?) Years in Egypt 1938-1526 B.C.
Moses 1526-1406 B.C.
Exodus from Egypt by Moses 1446 B.C.
Leadership by Joshua 1406-1381 B.C.
Judges of Israel 1381-1050 B.C.
United Kingdom 1050-910 B.C. **Under Saul/David/Solomon**
Divided Kingdom 931-586 B.C. **Israel and Judah**

The Fall of **Syria** 931 B.C.
The Fall of **Samaria** 722 B.C.
The Fall of **Assyria** 650 B.C.
The Fall of **Nineveh** 612 B.C.
1ˢᵗ Deportation of Jews 605 B.C.
2ⁿᵈ Deportation of Jews 597 B.C.
The Fall of **Jerusalem** 586 B.C.
The Fall of Babylon 539 B.C.
The Fall of **Persia** 331 B.C.
The Fall of **Greece** 323 B.C.
The Fall of **Egypt** 195 B.C.
The Fall of **Syria** 167 B.C.
The Fall of **Maccabees** 63 B.C.
The Fall of **Romans** 331 A.D.

THE KINGS OF THE DIVIDED KINGDOMS

Kings of Israel		Kings of Judah	
Jeroboam	933-911	Rehoboam	933-916
Nadab	911-910	Abijah	915-913
Baasha	910-887	Asa	912-872
Elah	887-886		
Zimri	886		
Omri	886-875		
Ahab	875-854	Jehoshaphat	874-850
Ahaziah	855-854	Jehoram	850-843
Joram	854-843	Ahaziah	843
Jehu	843-816	Athaliah	843-837
Jehoahaz	820-804	Joash	843-803
Jehoash	806-790	Amaziah	803-775
Jerboam II	790-749	Uzziah	787-735
Zechariah	748		
Shallum	748		
Menaem	748-738		
Pekahiah	738-736	Ahaz	741-726
Pekah	748-730		
Hoshea	730-721	Hezekiah	726-697
		Manasseh	697-642
		Amon	641-640
		Josiah	639-608
		Jehoahaz	608
		Jehoiakim	608-597
		Jehoiachin	597
		Zedekiah	597-586

Sample of Study Guide Two

THE LIFE OF MOSES
The Deliverer of Israel

We have laid the foundation of the Bible covering some 2300 years. We now come to the book of Exodus.

This book covers a time span of 120 years. From 1526 the birth of Moses until 1406 B.C. the death of Moses.

Moses is the most known bible character other than Jesus Christ. Other important characters of the Exodus are Aaron and Joshua.

The major events of the book are: the captivity of Israel, the deliverance of Israel, the giving of the Law to Israel and the building of the Tabernacle.

Within this study one will learn of the _Sacrificial Lamb for Individual God-followers and the Sacrificial Lamb for a Nation of God-followers._

A SIMPLE DIVISION OF THE BOOK OF EXODUS

Chapters 1-11 A Helpless Nation
Chapters 12-13 A Delivered Nation
Chapters 14-18 An Obedient Nation
Chapters 19-24 A Chosen Nation
Chapters 25-40 A Worshipping Nation

Historical Background of Exodus

A period of three hundred and three years had elapsed since the influence of God Follower Joseph had diminished. A new pharaoh (Amenhotep I), who knew not Joseph was ruling.

When Jacob entered Egypt, there were only seventy Hebrews. At this date the Hebrews numbered over three million, one-third of the population of Egypt. This new pharaoh feared that the Hebrews might revolt and take over. He sought to eliminate this problem by having all male Hebrew children killed at birth. Moses' parents sought to save the baby's life. They hid him at home until he became too noisy (probably teething). They placed the baby in a basket, in the Nile, near the place where the pharoah's daughter bathed. They watched and made sure he was found. When her handmaids heard the baby, they brought him to her. She saw that he was a healthy baby, several months old, she took him in as her own son. She named the baby Moses, (meaning drawn out).